copy & cut

Stories from Around the World

Paul Johnson

A & C Black • London

First published 2004 by A & C Black Publishers Ltd
37 Soho Square, London W1D 3QZ
www.acblack.com

ISBN 0-7136-6809-1

Copyright project ideas © Paul Johnson, 2004
Copyright illustrations © Kirsty Wilson, 2004
Copyright cover illustration © Alex Ayliffe, 2004
Teachers' notes and stories retold by Anita Ganeri
Editor: Lucy Poddington
Designer: Sharyn Troughton

A CIP catalogue record for this book is available
from the British Library.

Printed in Great Britain by Martins the Printers Ltd,
Berwick upon Tweed.

A & C Black uses paper produced with elemental
chlorine-free pulp, harvested from managed
sustainable forests.

Contents

Introduction

How to use this book

Copy and Cut: Stories from Around the World provides a wide variety of photocopiable craft templates, each with simple instructions for children to follow. The templates enable children to make books and models based on traditional stories from countries around the world. The projects provide innovative contexts for practising writing and literacy skills. There are opportunities for the children to read instructions, to write text for a purpose and to tell stories orally. The projects link with fiction and poetry work on traditional stories; stories about fantasy worlds; stories and poems from other cultures; and myths, legends, fables and parables.

The projects are designed for six to eight year-olds, but many are also suitable for younger or older children. Any project can be easily adapted to your needs by masking and/or substituting text. The pages are perforated so that favourite templates can be removed from the book and filed with other relevant resources. At the back of the book you will find photocopiable story texts of less well-known stories for children to read and use. There are also notes for teachers which include practical suggestions and additional information on the featured stories.

Preparation

First pull out the template page and cut around the border. Use this master page for all future photocopying (for a more exact copy, lay the page on the photocopier plate rather than feeding it in). To begin a project, photocopy both sides of the template for each child and check that the necessary resources are available (see 'You will need' for individual projects). Introduce the theme and discuss ideas for the project with the whole class. If necessary, read the instructions with the children and demonstrate what they mean. It is particularly useful to show the children how to hold the page to start with. A photocopiable page of helpful hints is provided on page 60.

Decorating the projects

The templates can be reproduced on white or coloured paper or card, either as A4 or enlarged to A3. A3 is a particularly useful size for demonstration purposes and for projects which involve substantial amounts of writing. The instructions suggest only basic decorating materials, such as coloured pencils, to avoid requests for materials that may not be available. However, it would be useful to start a collection of extra resources, so that children can be more adventurous with their decorations. Suitable materials include glitter glue, pearlised paints, metallic pens and paper, coloured foil paper, sequin mesh, tinsel, holographic paper, art straws, sweet papers, wrapping paper, magazines, fabric and wool.

Tips for good results

Encourage the children to try out decoration ideas on a piece of scrap paper first, and to plan in pencil. It's a good idea to avoid the use of fibre-tipped pens, as colours may run through the paper.

If you copy the template onto card, show the children how to score along the dots with a pencil and ruler before folding. You could consider making two copies of the template for each child. One can be used for the rough draft and the other for the finished piece.

The children could word-process texts and stick them onto their finished models or books.

Ideas for display

These projects are perfect for school displays. Why not mount projects together on a classroom wall or in the school hall?

The Sword in the Stone

A great sword was firmly stuck in a huge stone. Whoever pulled it out would become king of England! A boy called Arthur saw the sword in the stone and tried to pull it out. Write what happened next on your model.

You will need: the Sword in the Stone template • scissors • glue • pencil • pencil crayons and sweet wrappers for decorating

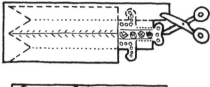
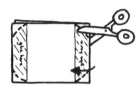

1. Cut along all the A dashes. Then cut along all the dashes on the sword.

2. Fold the other piece of paper in half widthways, like this. Cut along all the dashes. Unfold.

3. Spread glue where marked. Fold the paper in half with the glue inside. Press firmly.

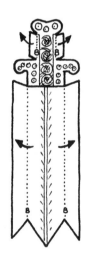

4. Fold the sword backwards along all the B dots.

5. Slide the sword into the stone.

On the stone, write the story of Arthur and the sword in the stone. Then decorate the sword using pencil crayons. You could glue sweet wrappers onto the handle for jewels.

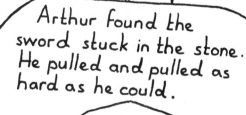
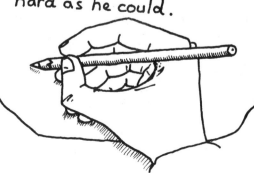

Arthur found the sword stuck in the stone. He pulled and pulled as hard as he could.

A
A
B
B
glue here
B
B
A
glue here
A

The Sword in the Stone template

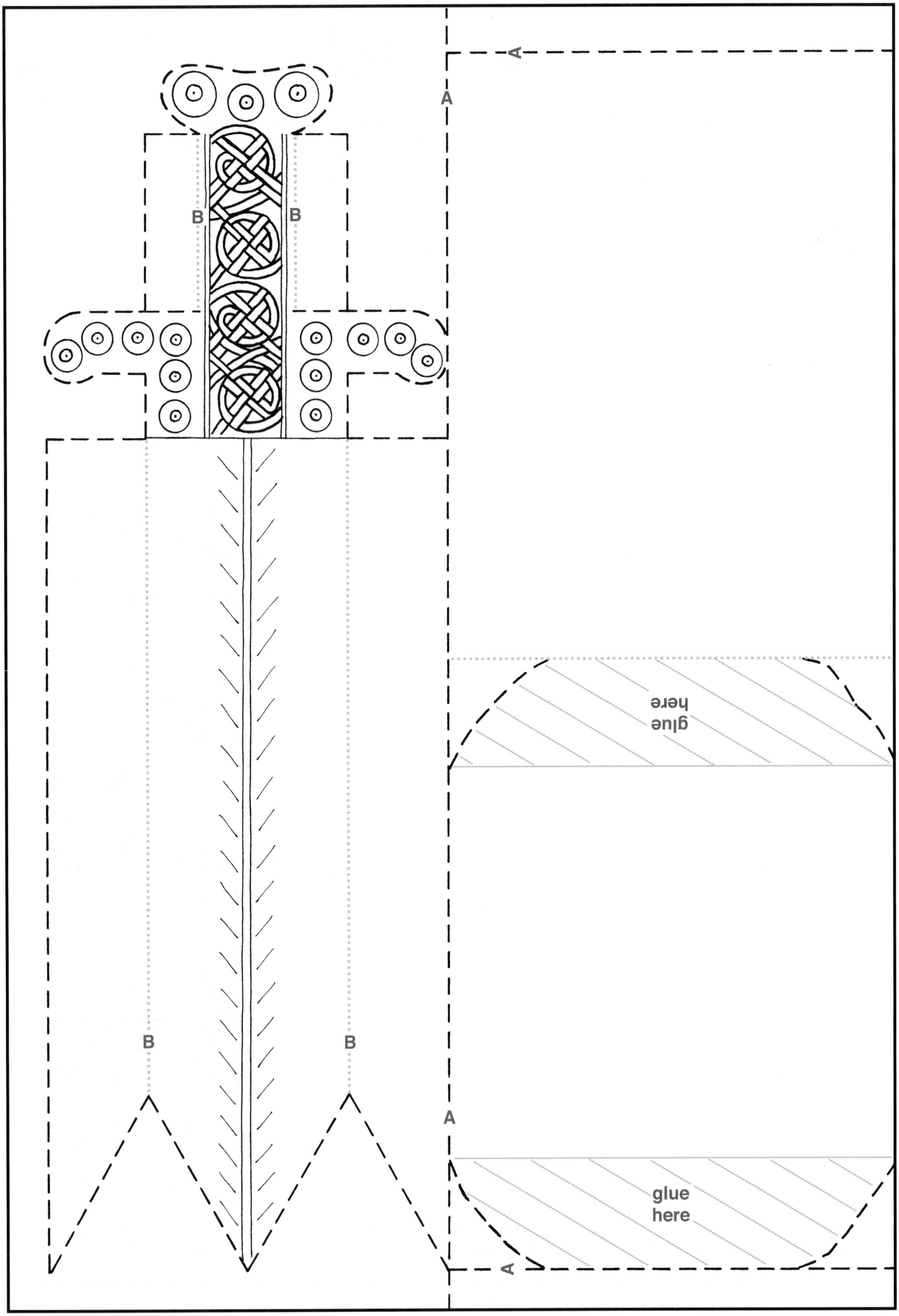

Beowulf

In this Old English story, Beowulf kills a fierce dragon which attacks his kingdom. Make this model of the dreadful creature. Decorate its skin to look like dragons' scales.

You will need: the Beowulf template • scissors • glue • pencil • pencil crayons for decorating

1. Decorate the paper. Then fold it in half lengthways, like this. Cut along all the dashes. Unfold the paper.

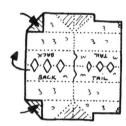

2. Fold backwards along the A dots. Fold the 'glue here' triangles forwards, like this. Then fold them backwards. Open out the paper.

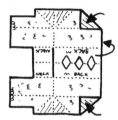

3. Fold backwards along the B dots. Fold the 'glue here' triangles forwards, like this. Then fold them backwards. Open out the paper.

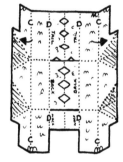

4. Fold backwards along all the C dots. Unfold. Do the same along all the D dots.

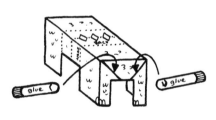

5. Spread glue on the triangles marked 'glue here'. Then fold the triangles together so that your model looks like this.

6. Spread glue on the inside of the dragon's back and tail. Lift them up, like this. Press the glued parts together.

7. Spread glue on the blank side of the dragon's head. Fasten it around the dragon's neck, like this.

On another piece of paper, list words to describe your dragon. Then tell a friend what happened when Beowulf met the dragon. Use your model to help you tell the story.

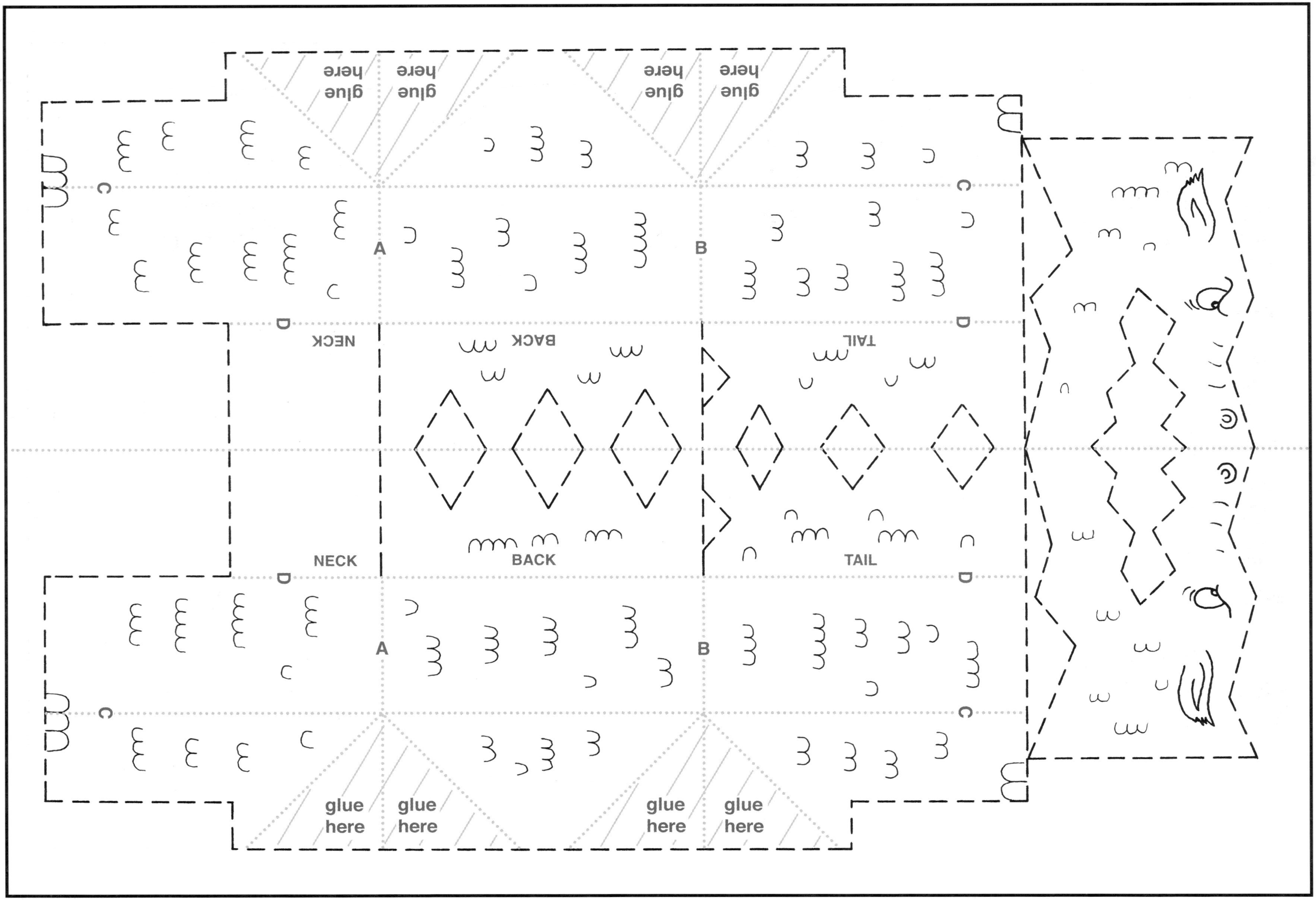

C D TAIL TAIL D C

glue here glue here glue here glue here

B B

glue here glue here glue here glue here

BACK BACK

A A

NECK NECK

D D

C C

The Poor Fisherman

A poor fisherman catches a magic fish which grants him three wishes. What do you think his greedy wife makes him wish for? Tell this story from Germany in your book. Draw pictures of the wishes under the flaps.

You will need: the Poor Fisherman template • the story of The Poor Fisherman (page 55) • scissors • pencil • pencil crayons for decorating

1. Fold the paper in half lengthways, like this.

2. Fold the paper in a zig-zag along the dashes (A, B, C). Start by folding forwards along the A dashes.

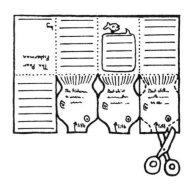

3. Open out the paper fully. Cut along all the dashes.

4. Fold the paper in half lengthways again.

5. Fold the book in a zig-zag.

Read the story. Then open out your book. On the first page, write about the fisherman catching the fish. Then lift the flaps. Draw the things the fisherman's wife wishes for. You could make up new things. Finish the story on the back three pages. Don't forget to draw a picture on the front cover.

But she still wasn't happy, so she made him wish for...

But she still wasn't happy, so she made him wish for...

The fisherman's wife made him wish for...

lift

C

B

A

The Poor Fisherman

by

Yggdrasil

The Vikings believed that a huge tree called Yggdrasil held up the earth. At the bottom lay a dragon and at the top was an eagle. They were deadly enemies! Write the insults that the squirrel carried between the two enemies.

You will need: the Yggdrasil template • scissors • glue • pencil • pencil crayons for decorating

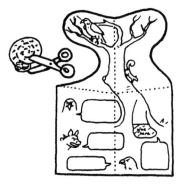

1. Cut along all the dashes. Colour the tree and both sides of the dragon.

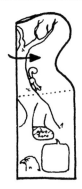

2. Fold the paper in half lengthways, like this.

3. Fold forwards along the A dots. Then fold backwards. Open out the paper.

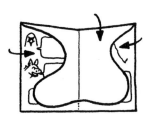

4. Carefully fold the top half forwards along the A dots. At the same time, fold the paper forwards to make a card.

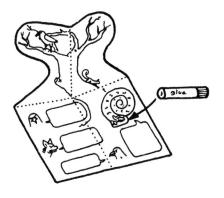

5. Unfold the paper. Spread glue where marked on the card. Place the dragon's head on the glue, like this.

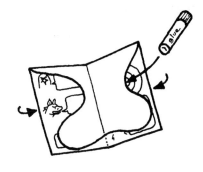

6. Spread glue on the dragon's tail. Close the card and leave it to dry.

Open the card and lift up the tree. Gently bend the fold in the base the other way, to make the tree stand up.

What insults might the eagle send to the dragon? Think about what a dragon looks and sounds like. Write the insults in the speech bubbles. Then make up the insults that the dragon sends to the eagle.

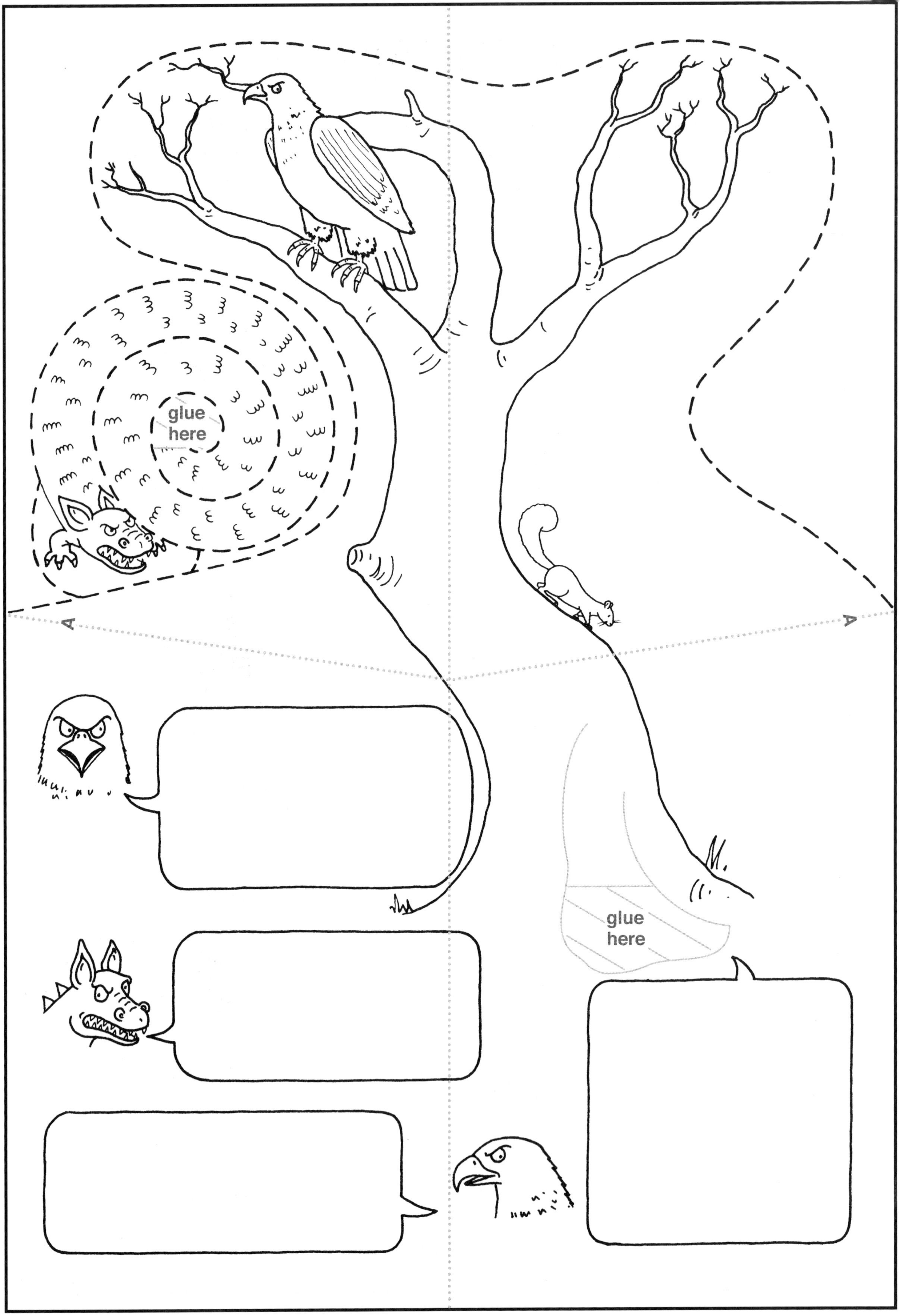

glue here

glue here

A

A

The North Wind and the Sun

In this story from Greece, the North Wind and the Sun quarrel about which of them is the stronger. Read the story and find out what happens. Talk about the moral with a friend and write the story in this book.

You will need: the North Wind and the Sun template • the story of The North Wind and the Sun (page 55) • scissors • pencil • pencil crayons for decorating

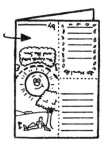

1. Fold the paper in half widthways, like this.

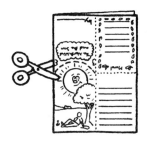

2. Cut along the dashes. Unfold.

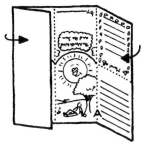

3. Fold the paper forwards along all the A dots. Unfold.

4. Fold the paper backwards along all the B dots.

5. Push the left and right edges towards each other, so that you make a box shape in the middle. Keep pushing until the sides touch.

6. Fold the front and back covers around the other pages.

Read the story. Then look at the pictures in your book. Use the story to help you decide what you will write for each picture. Write the moral of the story at the end.

I'm stronger than you.

No you're not. I bet you can't make that man take off his coat.

Androcles and the Lion

Long ago, a Greek slave ran away from his cruel master. When he was caught, he was thrown to a lion. But instead of eating him, the lion licked his hand. Do you know why? Read the story to find out.

You will need: the Androcles and the Lion template • the story of Androcles and the Lion (page 56) • scissors • pencil • pencil crayons for decorating

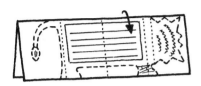

1. Fold the paper in half lengthways, like this.

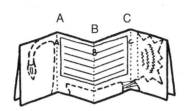

2. Fold the paper in a zig-zag along the dots (A, B, C). Start by folding forwards along the A dots.

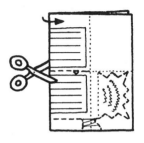

3. Open the paper fully. Then fold it in half widthways, like this. Cut along the D dashes. Unfold.

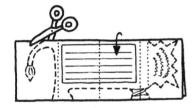

4. Fold the paper in half lengthways. Cut along all the dashes.

5. Fold the lion's head open along the E dots. Draw the lion's face.

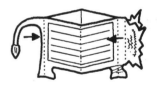

6. Push the left and right edges towards each other, so that you make a box shape in the middle.

Press your model flat. Write the story of Androcles and the Lion in your own words. Begin the story on the front of the lion and finish it on the back. Decorate your model using pencil crayons.

Pandora's Box

When Pandora opened a magic box, she let out terrible evils into the world. But a tiny fairy also flew out. Her name was Hope and she brought hope for the future. Write this Greek story on your own box.

You will need: the Pandora's Box template • scissors • glue • pencil • pencil crayons and glitter for decorating

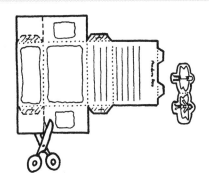

1. Cut along all the dashes. Write the story on the paper. Decorate both sides of the paper using pencil crayons.

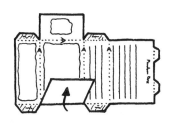

2. Fold the paper forwards along the A dots, like this. Unfold. Do the same along all the other A dots.

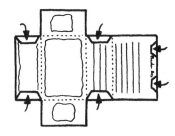

3. Fold the tabs forwards along all the B dots. Unfold.

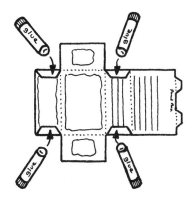

4. Spread glue on the back of the four tabs, where marked.

5. Fold the paper along the creases to make a box. Fasten the tabs inside the box.

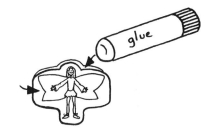

6. Fold the fairy in half along the dots, like this. Spread glue inside and press the two halves together.

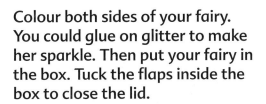

Colour both sides of your fairy. You could glue on glitter to make her sparkle. Then put your fairy in the box. Tuck the flaps inside the box to close the lid.

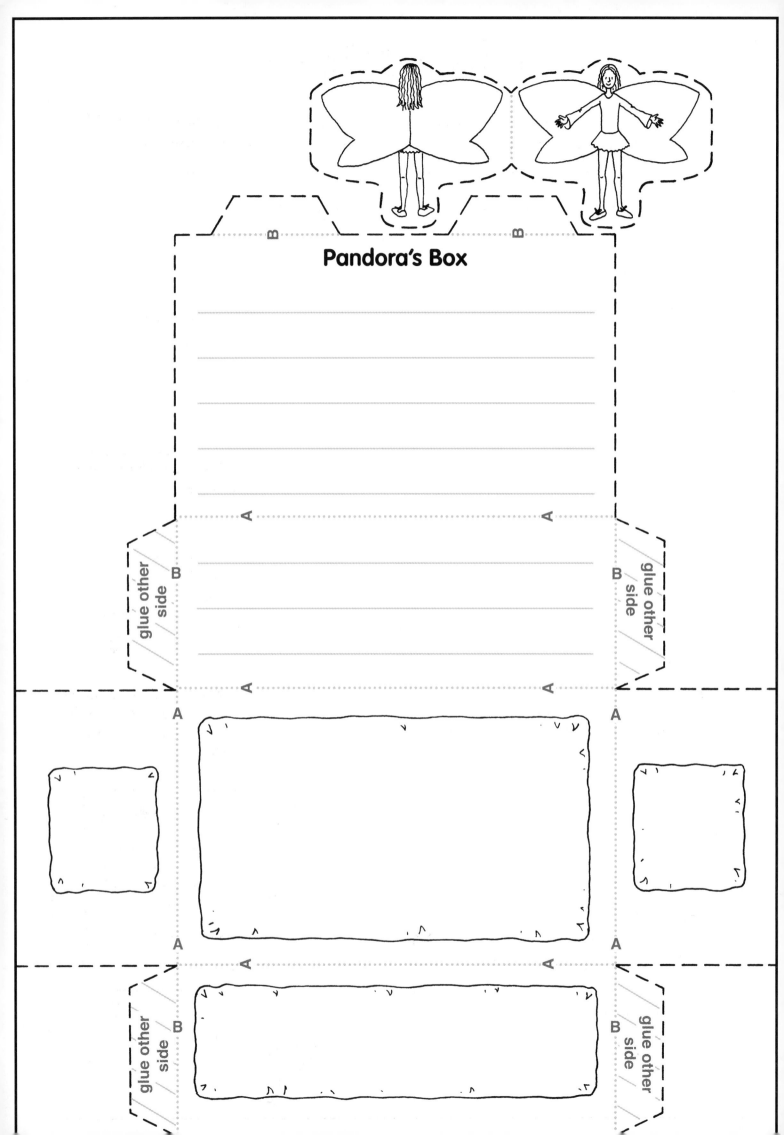

Pandora's Box

glue other side

glue other side

glue other side

glue other side

King Midas

In this Greek legend, King Midas wished that everything he touched would turn to gold. Do you know what happened when the wish came true? You can tell the story yourself in this pop-up book.

You will need: the King Midas template • scissors • glue • pencil • pencil crayons for decorating

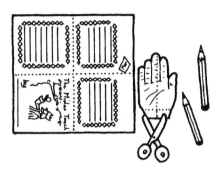

1. Cut along all the dashes. Turn the hand over and draw the fingers and fingernails.

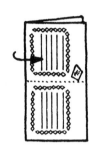

2. Fold the paper along the A dots, like this.

3. Now fold along the B dots, like this. Write the story in your book.

4. Fold the hand in half, with the marks on the inside. Fold tab A forwards along the dots.

5. Spread glue on Tab A. Then place it on your book where marked.

6. Fold Tab B forwards along the dots. Spread glue on the tab. Close your book and leave it to dry.

Write your name on the front of your book and colour the picture. When you open the book to read the story, King Midas's hand will pop out!

21

TAB
A

TAB
B

PLACE
TAB A
HERE

A

B

The Midas Touch

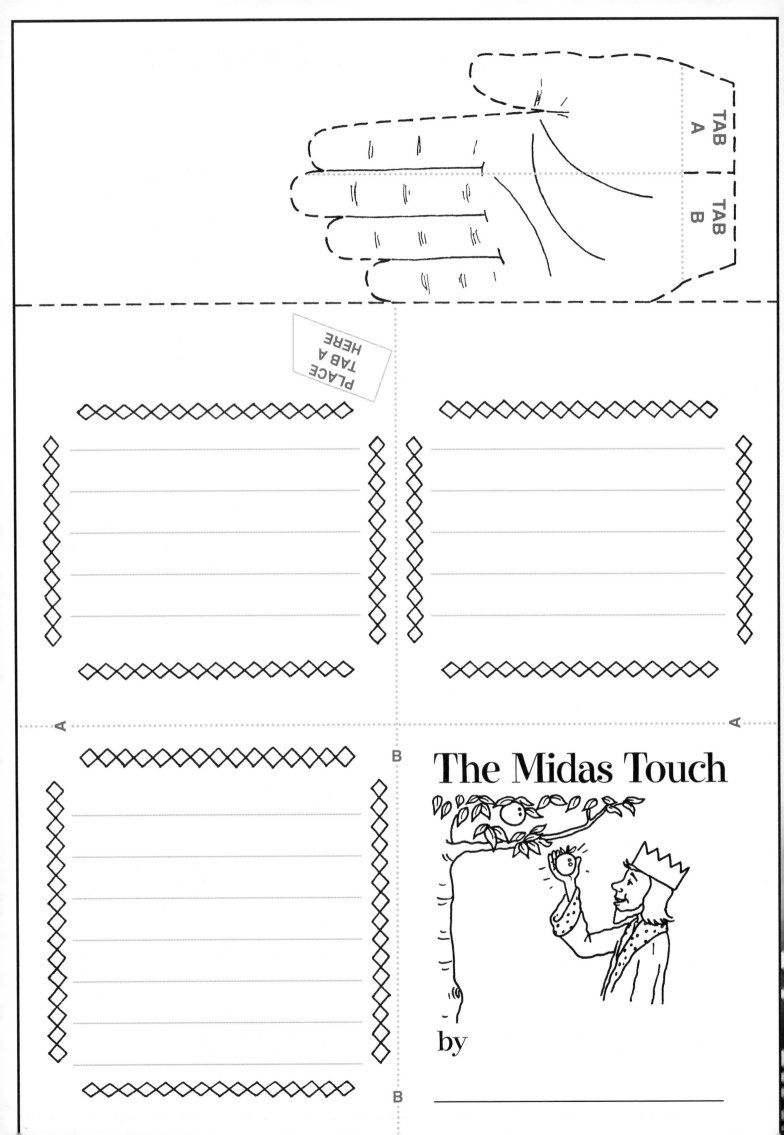

by

_____

Atlantis – the Magical Island

The ancient Greeks told stories about a beautiful island called Atlantis. One day, the island suddenly sank into the sea. Do you think the island ever really existed? On your model, show what you think it might have looked like.

You will need: the Atlantis — the Magical Island template • scissors • pencil • pencil crayons, silver paper and glue for decorating

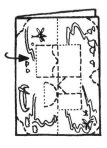

1. Fold the paper in half widthways, like this.

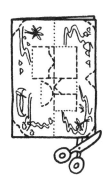

2. Cut along all the dashes at the edges. Unfold.

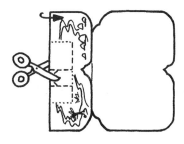

3. Fold the paper backwards along the A dots and dashes. Cut along the B dashes only. Unfold.

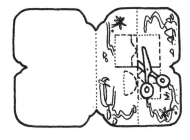

4. Cut along all the other dashes.

5. Fold the paper in half widthways again. Fold the flaps along the dots to make them stand up.

Press your model flat and draw buildings on the flaps. There might be splendid palaces, towers and wonderful temples. Colour the rest of the picture.

Then lift the flaps and draw the back of each building. Draw a lake in the space in the middle. You could glue on pieces of silver paper for water.

23

Medusa

In Greek myths, Medusa was a monster who had wriggling snakes instead of hair. If you dared to look into her eyes, you would be turned to stone! Make this scary mask to wear when you tell the story.

You will need: the Medusa template • scissors • glue • hole puncher • a length of elastic • pencil • pencil crayons, glitter and foil for decorating

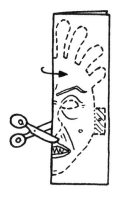

1. Fold the paper in half lengthways, like this. Cut along all the dashes. Unfold.

2. Turn the mask over. Fold the tabs along the dots. Then unfold.

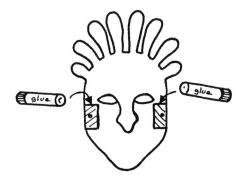

3. Spread glue on the back of the tabs and glue them to the mask.

4. Use a hole puncher to make holes in the circles.

5. Cut a length of elastic to fit your head. Tie it through the holes.

6. Gently curl each snake forwards around a pencil. Then use a pencil to curl each snake's head the other way.

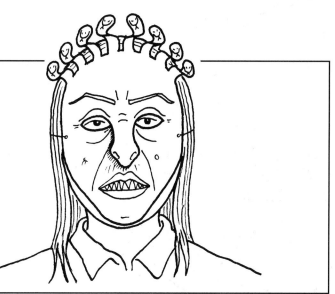

Colour the mask. Then glue glitter and foil onto the snakes. Make them look as scary as you can.

Now make notes about the story of Medusa. What did she look like? What happened to her? Put on the mask and tell the story to a friend.

25

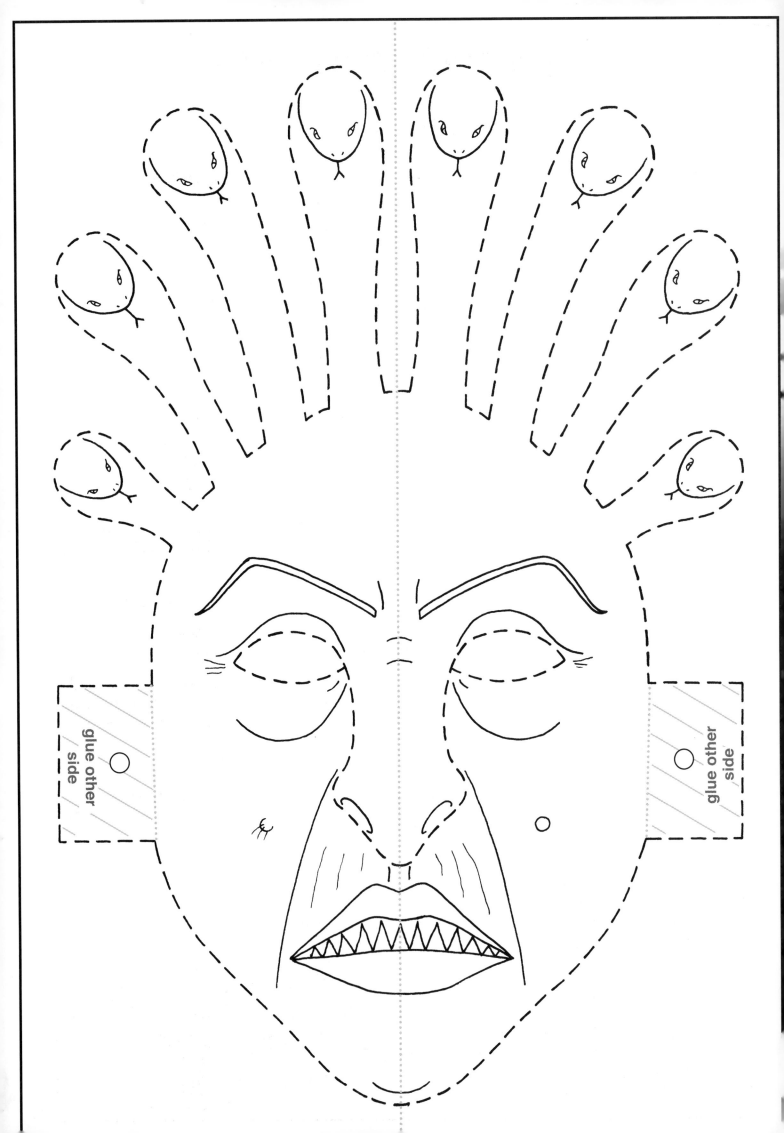

glue other side ○

glue other side ○

Habeeb and the Flying Carpet

Once upon a time in Asia, a boy called Habeeb had a magic carpet. It took him wherever he wanted to go. Where would you go if you could fly anywhere? What would you do? Write your ideas on this carpet.

You will need: the Habeeb and the Flying Carpet template
- the story of Habeeb and the Flying Carpet (page 56)
- scissors • glue • pencil • pencil crayons for decorating

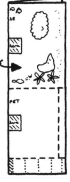

1. Fold the paper in half lengthways, like this. Unfold.

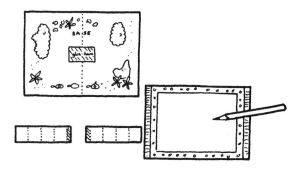

2. Cut along all the dashes. Decorate the blank side of the carpet and write about where you would like to go. Then colour the base.

3. Take one of the small strips. Fold backwards along the A dots. Unfold. Then do the same along all the other dots.

4. Spread glue where marked. Fasten it to the other end of the strip to make a box.

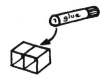

5. Repeat steps 3 and 4 with the other strip. Glue the two boxes together, like this.

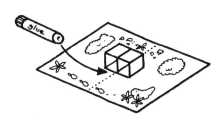

6. Spread glue on the base where marked. Place the boxes on the glued part.

7. Spread glue on the carpet where marked. Carefully place it on top of the boxes.

Read the story of Habeeb and the Flying Carpet. Draw tassels around the edge of your flying carpet. In the middle, write about where you would like to go. Fold your model forwards to close the pop-up.

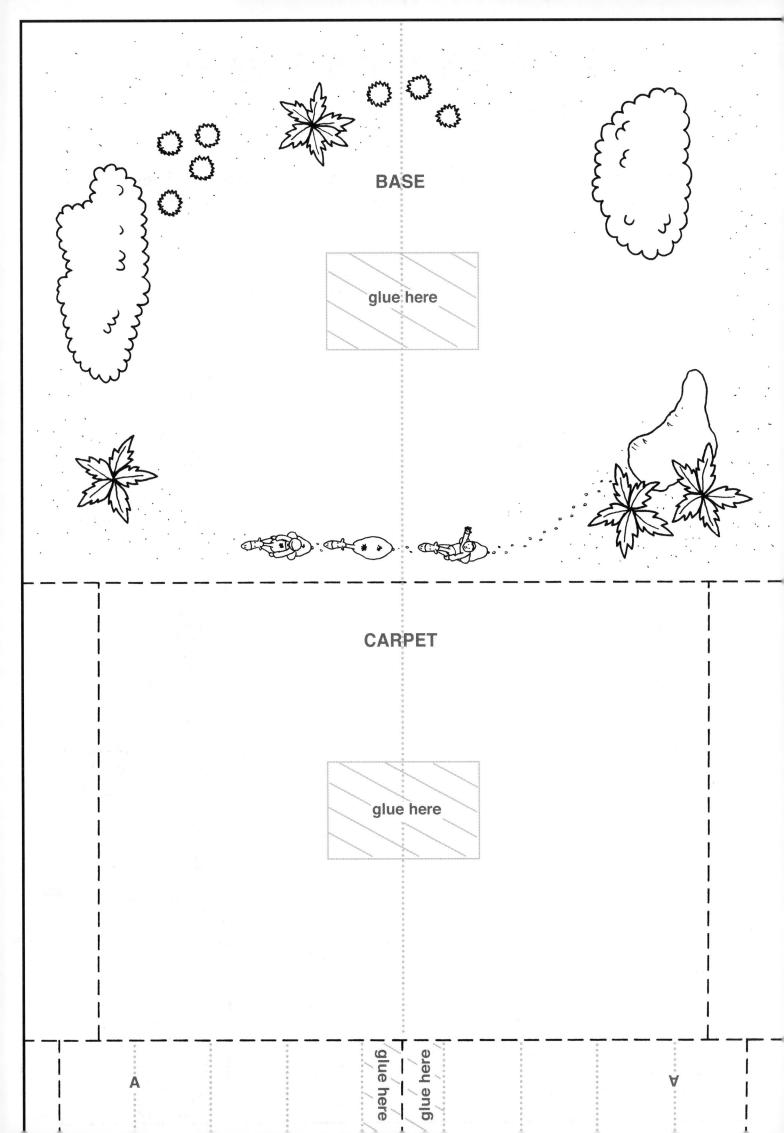

BASE

glue here

CARPET

glue here

glue here

glue here

A

A

Ali Baba and the Forty Thieves

In this story from the Middle East, forty thieves hid inside forty jars. They wanted to attack Ali Baba. Read the story to find out what happened next.
Make a sneaky thief pop up out of this jar.

You will need: the Ali Baba and the Forty Thieves template
• the story of Ali Baba and the Forty Thieves (page 57)
• scissors • glue • pencil • pencil crayons for decorating

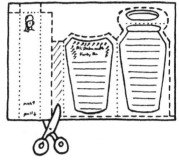

1. Cut along all the dashes.

2. Fold the paper backwards along the A dots. Then fold backwards along the B dots.

3. Spread glue on the tab and fasten it inside the jar.

4. Turn the jar over. Fold forwards along the C dots. Unfold.

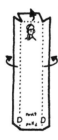

5. Fold the long strip backwards along all the D dots. Then fold backwards along the E dots.

6. Slide the strip into the jar. Spread glue on the tab and fasten it to the crease on the jar lid, like this.

Read the story of Ali Baba and the Forty Thieves. Write the story in your own words on the jar. Use the front and the back.

Then colour the thief inside the jar. Pull the tab down to close the jar lid. Push it back up to see the thief pop up.

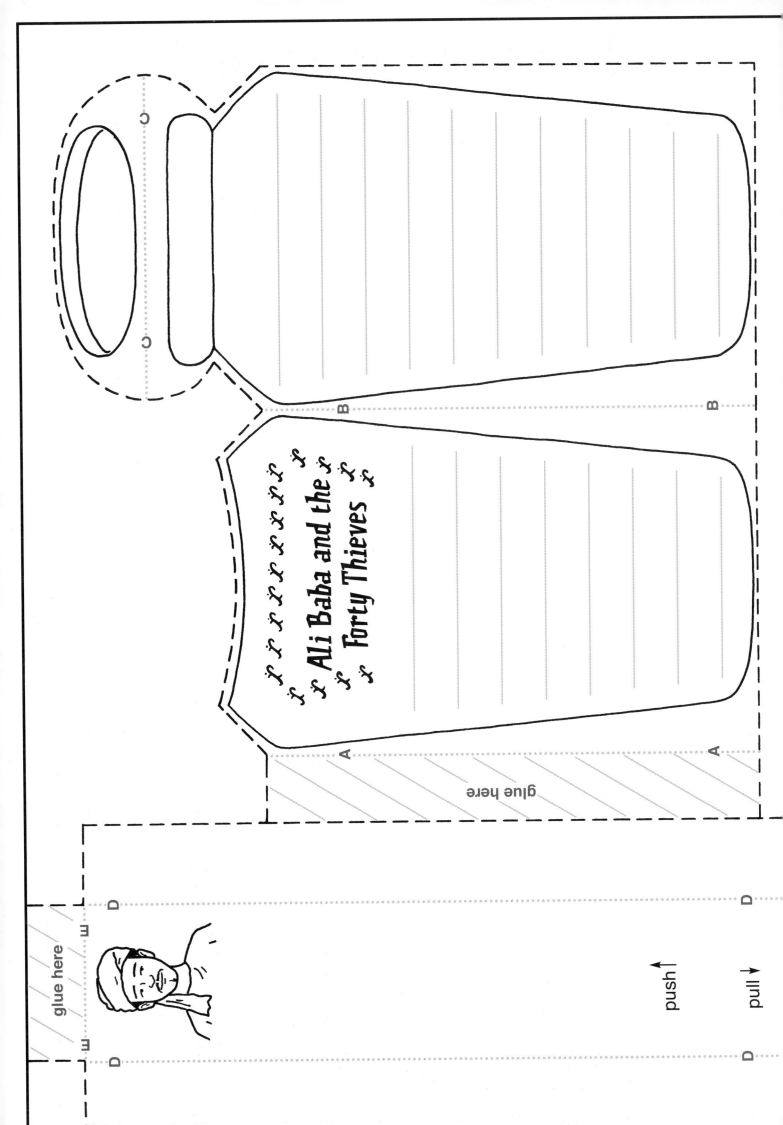

Ali Baba and the Forty Thieves

glue here

glue here

push

pull

The Clever Jackal

Once upon a time in India, a clever jackal helped a poor weaver to marry a rich and beautiful princess. Read the story, then think of another amazing adventure for the clever jackal to have.

You will need: the Clever Jackal template • the story of The Clever Jackal (page 57) • scissors • pencil • pencil crayons for decorating

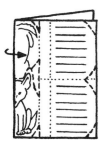

1. Fold the paper in half widthways, like this.

2. Cut along all the dashes. Unfold.

3. Fold the paper backwards along all the A dots.

4. Fold forwards along all the B dots. Unfold.

5. Fold backwards along all the C dots. Stand your model up.

Press your model flat. Write your own story about the clever jackal. Will he help the weaver again? Or will he help other animals?

Turn the model over and finish your story on the back. Colour in the picture of the jackal.

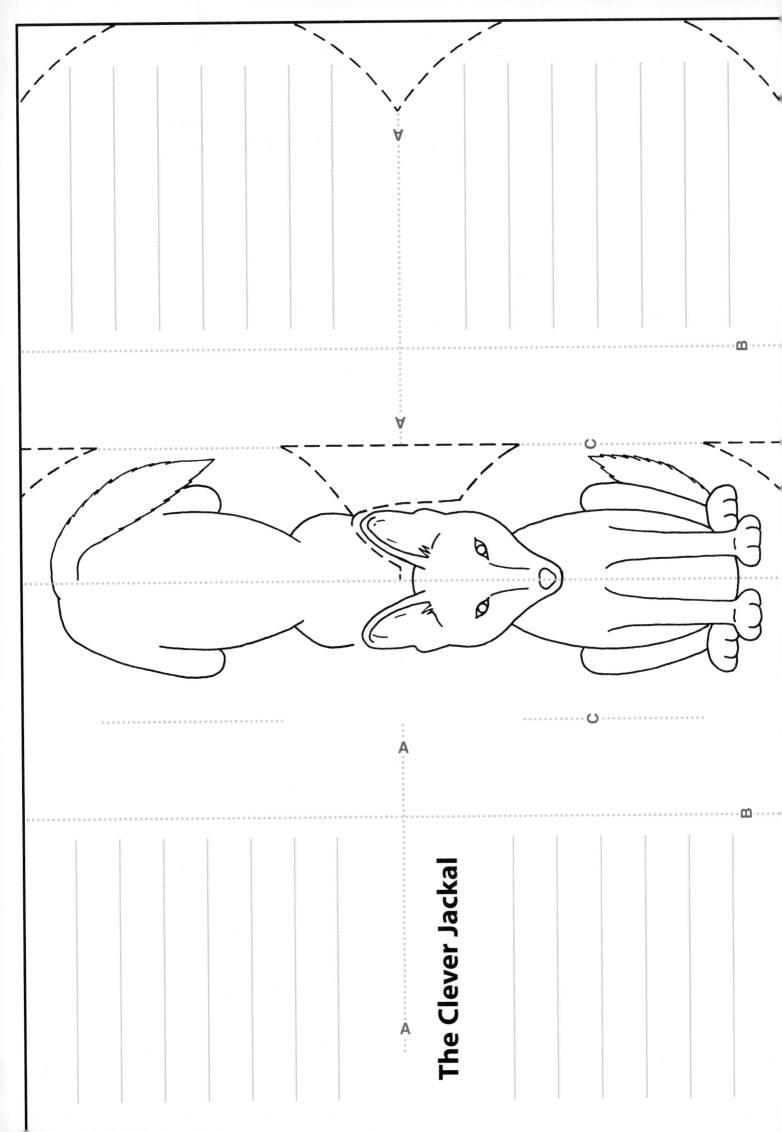

The Clever Jackal

The Magic Tea Bush

People in China tell a story about the very first cup of tea. Long ago, a sleepy old monk made a drink using leaves from the magic tea bush. The hot tea helped him to stay awake while he prayed. Make your own pop-up tea cup and saucer.

You will need: the Magic Tea Bush template • scissors • glue • pencil • pencil crayons for decorating

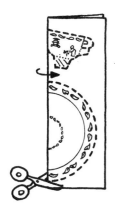

1. Fold the paper in half lengthways, like this. Cut along all the dashes. Unfold the shapes.

2. Decorate the cup. Then fold backwards along all the A dots.

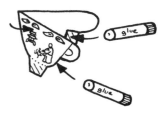

3. Spread glue where marked. Fold the cup in half and press the glued parts together.

4. Fold forwards along the B dots. Then fold backwards. Unfold.

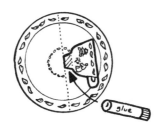

5. Spread glue on Tab C. Place it on the saucer where marked.

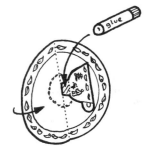

6. Spread glue on Tab D. Fold the saucer closed and press firmly. Leave to dry.

Decorate your cup and saucer in matching colours.

When the glue is dry, open the saucer and press it flat. Write the start of the story around the edge of the saucer.

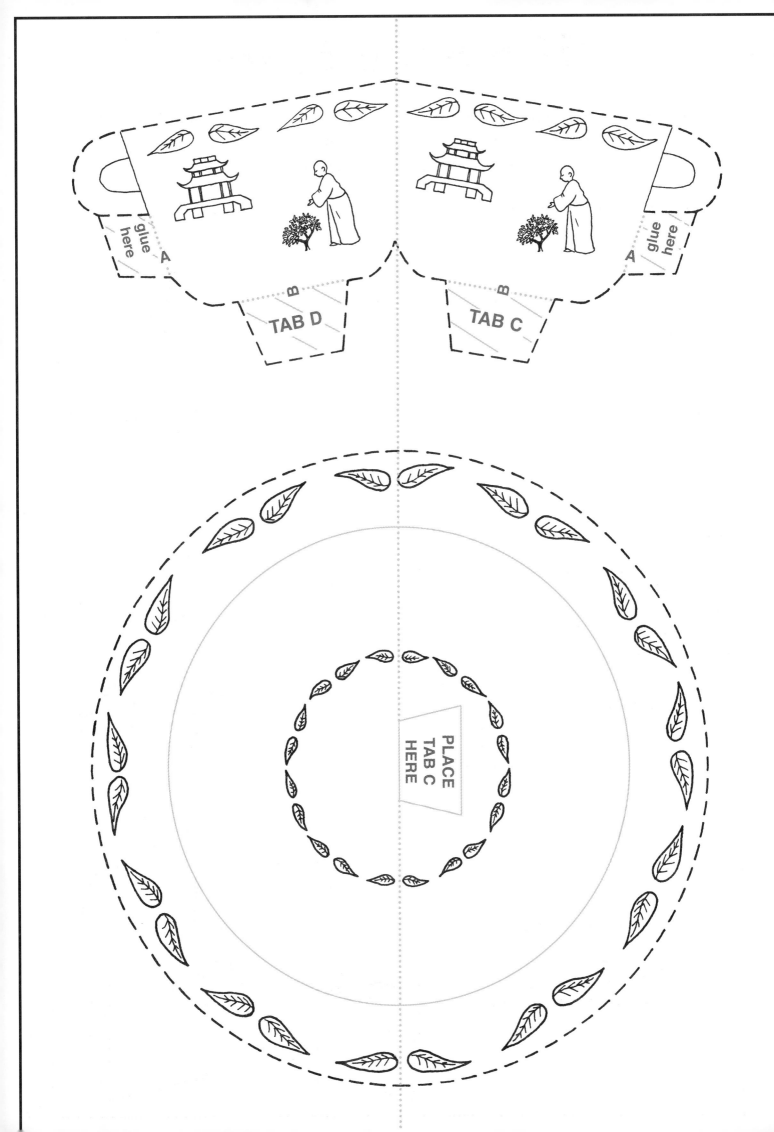

glue here

A

B

TAB D

glue here

A

B

TAB C

PLACE TAB C HERE

The Herb Fairy

High in the mountains of China, people believed that the herb fairy looked after the precious plants on the hillsides. Make this leaf-shaped book and use it to tell the story.

You will need: the Herb Fairy template • scissors • pencil • pencil crayons for decorating

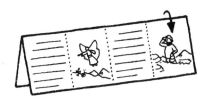

1. Fold the paper in half lengthways, like this.

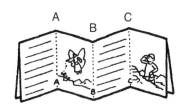

2. Fold the paper in a zig-zag along the dots (A, B, C). Start by folding forwards along the A dots.

3. Press the zig-zag flat. Cut along the dashes.

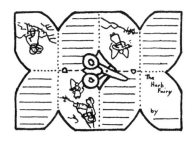

4. Open out the paper fully. Cut along the D dashes.

5. Fold the paper in half lengthways again. Push the left and right edges towards each other, so that you make a box shape in the middle.

6. Keep pushing until the sides touch. Find the front cover and fold it around all the other pages.

Look at the pictures in your book and decide what to write on each page. Write your story, then colour the pictures. Don't forget to write your name and draw a picture on the front cover.

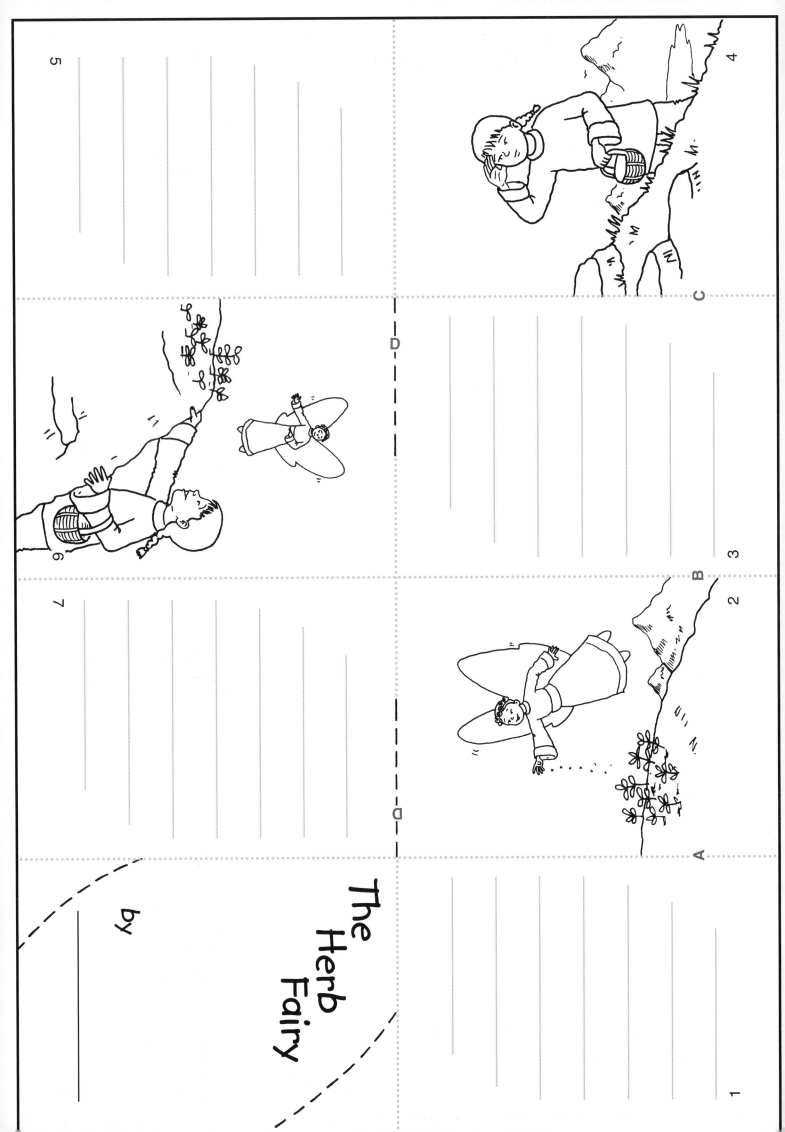

4

C

D

3

B

2

A

5

6

7

1

The Herb Fairy

by _____

The Sky God

A story from Africa tells how the sky god, Nyame, created the earth. He put plants and animals into a basket and lowered it to the ground.
Make this model to show the basket on its way down.

You will need: the Sky God template • scissors • glue • hole puncher • a piece of thread
• pencil • pencil crayons for decorating

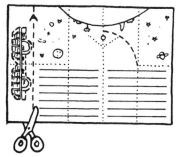

1. Cut along the A dashes. Then decorate the basket.

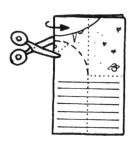

2. Fold the large piece of paper in half widthways. Cut along the dashes.

3. Fold forwards along the B dots. Then fold backwards. Unfold.

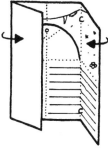

4. Open out the paper. Fold forwards along all the C dots. Unfold.

5. Fold backwards along the D dots. Stand the card up, like this. Gently fold forwards along the B dots.

6. Fold the basket in half along the dots. Then cut along the dashes.

7. Glue the basket together. Use a hole puncher to make a hole in the circle.

8. Make a hole in the top of the card. Loop a piece of thread through the holes and tie it.

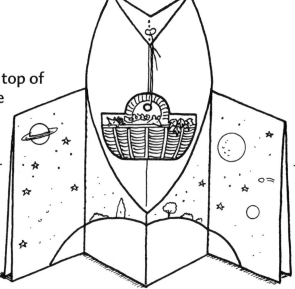

Press your model flat and colour the earth and the sky. Then turn it over. On the back, write the story of how the sky god created the earth.

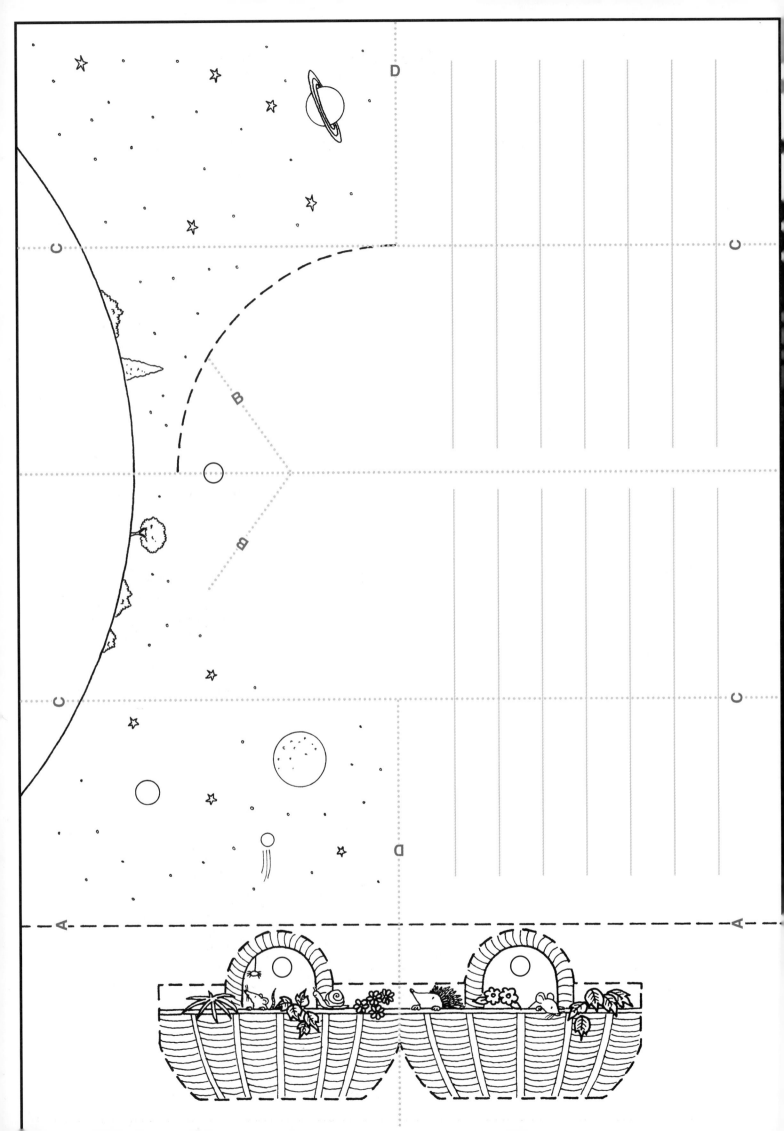

The Honey Bird

In a forest in Africa, the honey bird finds a tree where there is an enormous honeycomb. All the animals want to taste the sticky honey.
Read the story and make your own tree.

You will need: the Honey Bird template • the story of The Honey Bird (page 58) • scissors • pencil • glue • pencil crayons for decorating

1. Colour the honeycomb and the bird. Then cut them out.

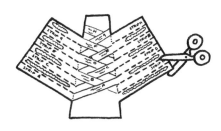

2. Cut out the tree. Then cut along all the dashes on the branches.

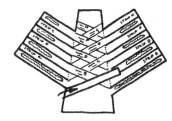

3. Fold Strip A forwards along the dots. Fit it onto the shape on the tree trunk.

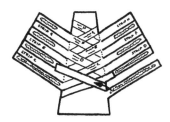

4. Now fold Strip B forwards over Strip A. Fit it onto the shape on the tree trunk.

5. Do the same with Strips C, D, E, F, G and H. Your tree should look like this.

6. Glue the honeycomb onto the branches, anywhere you like.

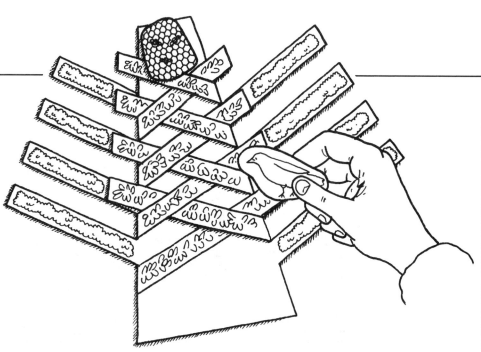

Colour your tree. Then re-read the story. Tell a friend what happens, in your own words. You can make the honey bird fly and land in the tree as you tell the story.

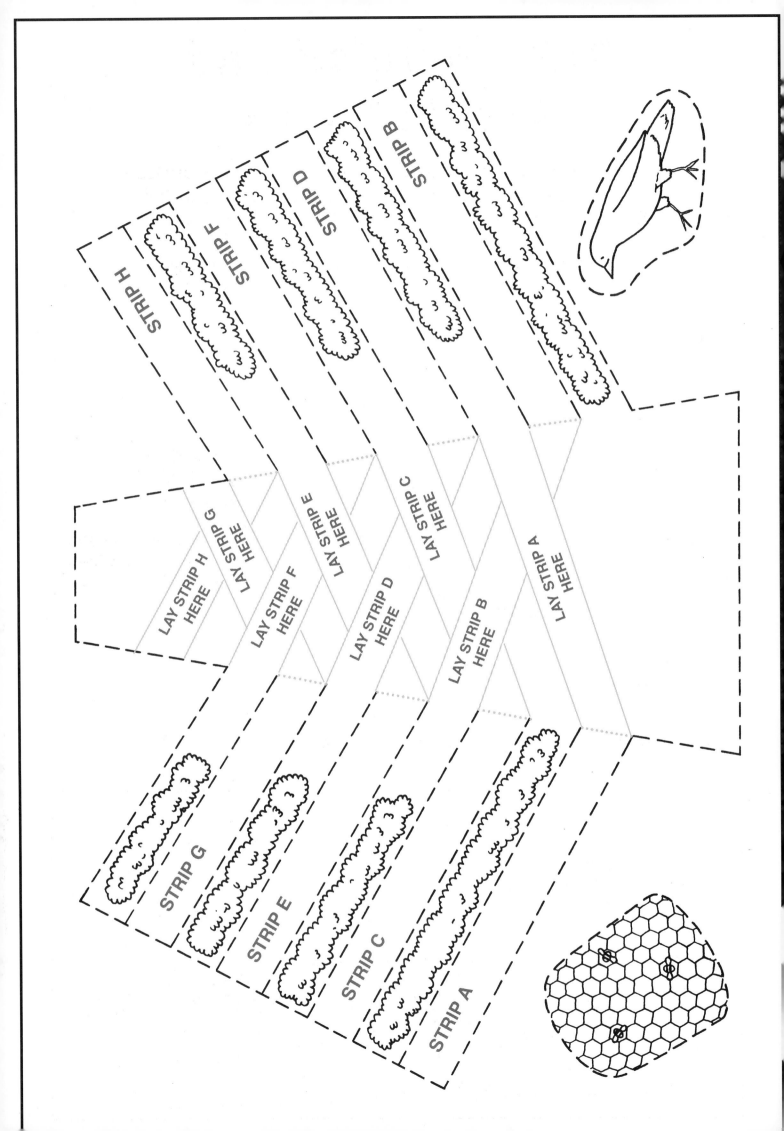

STRIP H

STRIP F

STRIP D

STRIP B

STRIP G

STRIP E

STRIP C

STRIP A

LAY STRIP H
HERE

LAY STRIP G
HERE

LAY STRIP F
HERE

LAY STRIP E
HERE

LAY STRIP D
HERE

LAY STRIP C
HERE

LAY STRIP B
HERE

LAY STRIP A
HERE

The Tortoise and the Leopard

In this African story, a lazy tortoise pretends to be a fierce, scary leopard.
How do people teach the tortoise a lesson? Read the story to find out.
Then make a model to show the tortoise in his clever disguise.

You will need: the Tortoise and the Leopard template • the story of The Tortoise and
the Leopard (page 58) • scissors • pencil • pencil crayons for decorating

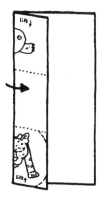

1. Start with the blank side facing you. Fold forwards along the A dots, like this.

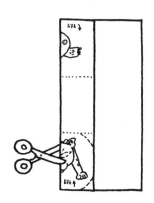

2. Cut along the dashes on the leopard's eyes.

3. Open out the paper. Then fold backwards along the B dots.

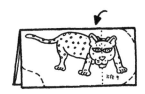

4. Now fold backwards along the C dots.

5. Cut along all the dashes.

Lift the leopard picture to see the tortoise hiding underneath. Then lift the tortoise and draw a picture to go with the story. You could draw the shopkeepers catching the tortoise. Write about what is happening in your picture.

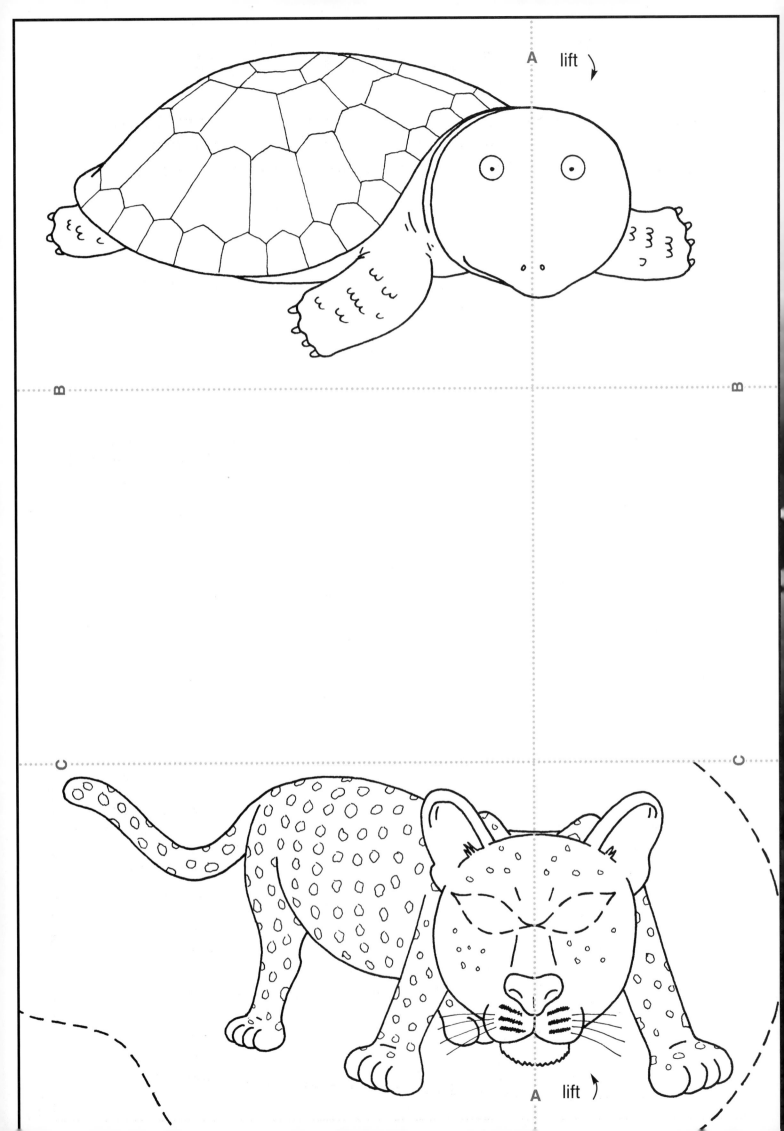

A lift ↘

B

B

C

C

A lift ↗

Ra, the Sun God

The ancient Egyptians worshipped a sun god called Ra. They thought that the sun was Ra sailing across the sky in his boat. Every evening he disappeared and in the morning he came back. You can show Ra's journey on this pop-up card.

You will need: the Ra, the Sun God template • scissors • pencil • pencil crayons for decorating

1. Fold the paper in half widthways, like this.

2. Cut along the dashes.

3. Fold the paper forwards along the A dots. Then fold backwards. Unfold.

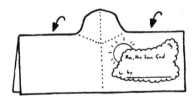

4. Open out the paper. Then fold backwards along the B dots.

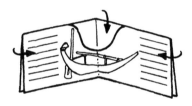

5. Turn the paper over. Gently fold forwards along the A dots and fold your card forwards to close it.

Open your card. At the sides of the picture, write about Ra, the Sun God. Describe his journey across the sky.

Now draw the sun on the pop-up. Close your card to watch the sun set. Then open it to see it rise again.

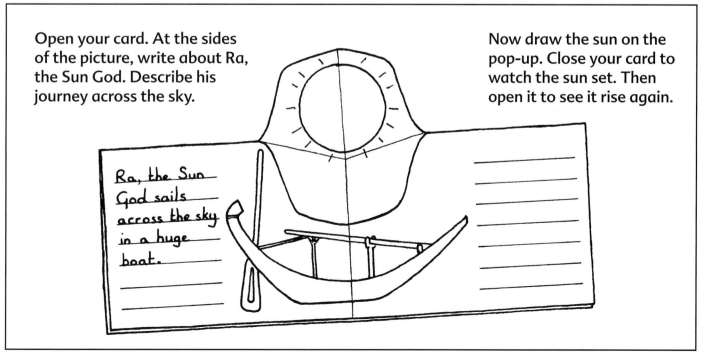

Ra, the Sun God sails across the sky in a huge boat.

Ra, the Sun God

by _____

The Heavenly Llama

People in South America told stories about a llama. Every night, it came down from heaven to drink. If the llama did not appear, the rivers overflowed and the villages were flooded. Write about the llama on this moving card.

You will need: the Heavenly Llama template • scissors • hole puncher • a split pin • pencil • pencil crayons for decorating

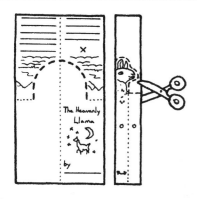

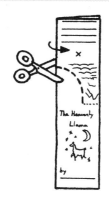

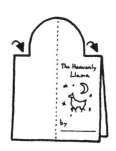

1. Cut along the A dashes. Then cut along the dashes around the llama's head. Put this strip to one side.

2. Fold the paper in half lengthways, like this. Cut along the dashes. Unfold.

3. Fold the paper backwards along the B dots.

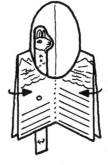

4. Fold the strip backwards along the dots. Use a hole puncher to make a hole in the circle.

5. Place the strip inside the card. Carefully push a split pin through the cross and the hole in the strip.

6. Open out the pin on the back of the strip. Fold the paper forwards to close your card.

Tell the story of The Heavenly Llama on your card. Then colour the llama and draw the sky behind it. Move the strip to see the llama drink. Don't forget to write your name on the cover.

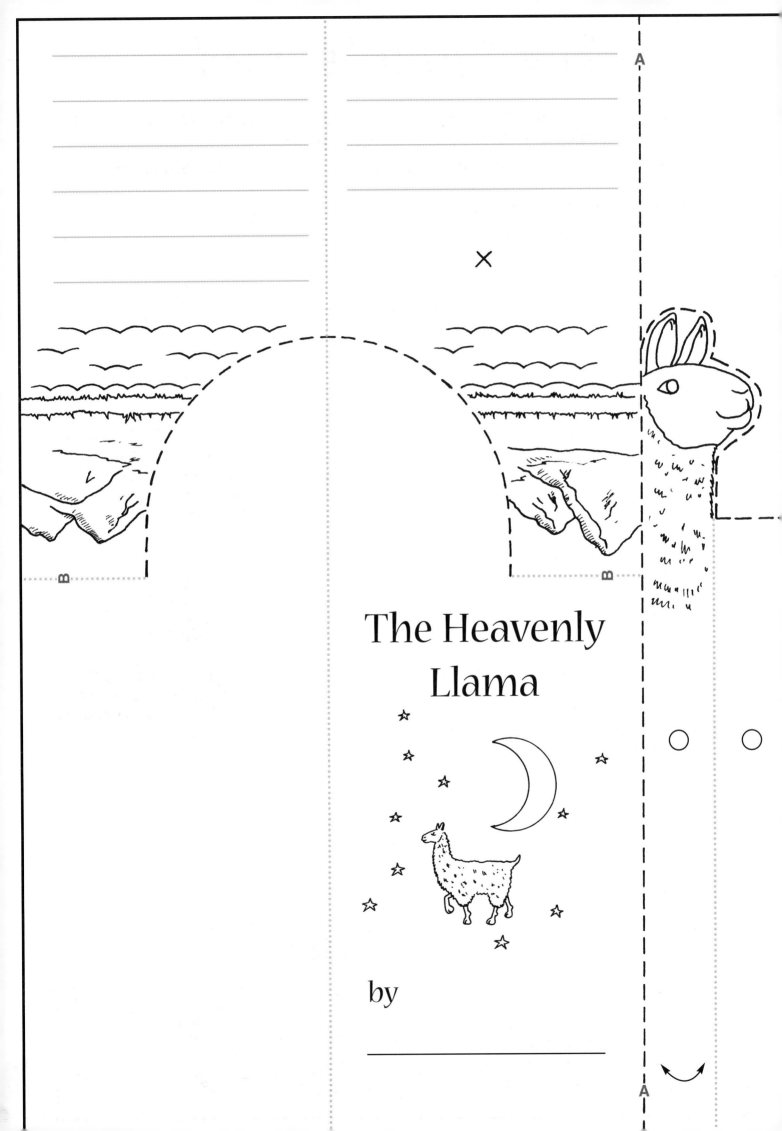

The Heavenly Llama

by

The Thunderbird

A Native American story tells how a giant eagle called the Thunderbird causes thunderstorms. Lightning flashes from its eyes and beak. The rumble of thunder is the beating of its wings. Make and decorate your own Thunderbird model.

You will need: the Thunderbird template • scissors • glue • pencil • pencil crayons for decorating

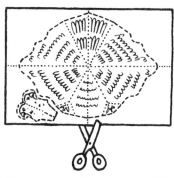

1. Decorate the paper. Then cut along all the dashes. Make sure you cut along the dashes on the bird's head.

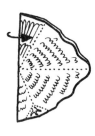

2. Fold the paper backwards along the A dots. Unfold. Then do the same along the B dots.

3. Fold the paper backwards along the C dots. Fold forwards along the D dots. Then fold backwards. Open out the paper.

4. Fold the paper backwards along the E dots. Fold forwards along the F dots. Then fold backwards. Open out the paper.

5. Fold forwards along the C dots. Unfold. Fold forwards along the E dots. Unfold.

6. Fold the paper along the B dots and gently push the wings downwards. Lift up the bird's feet.

7. Fold the bird's head in half, like this. Unfold. Then spread glue all over the blank side.

8. Fasten the bird's head onto the model. Press the glued parts together.

Tell the story of the Thunderbird to a friend. Describe what the bird looks like and what it sounds like. Use your model to help you.

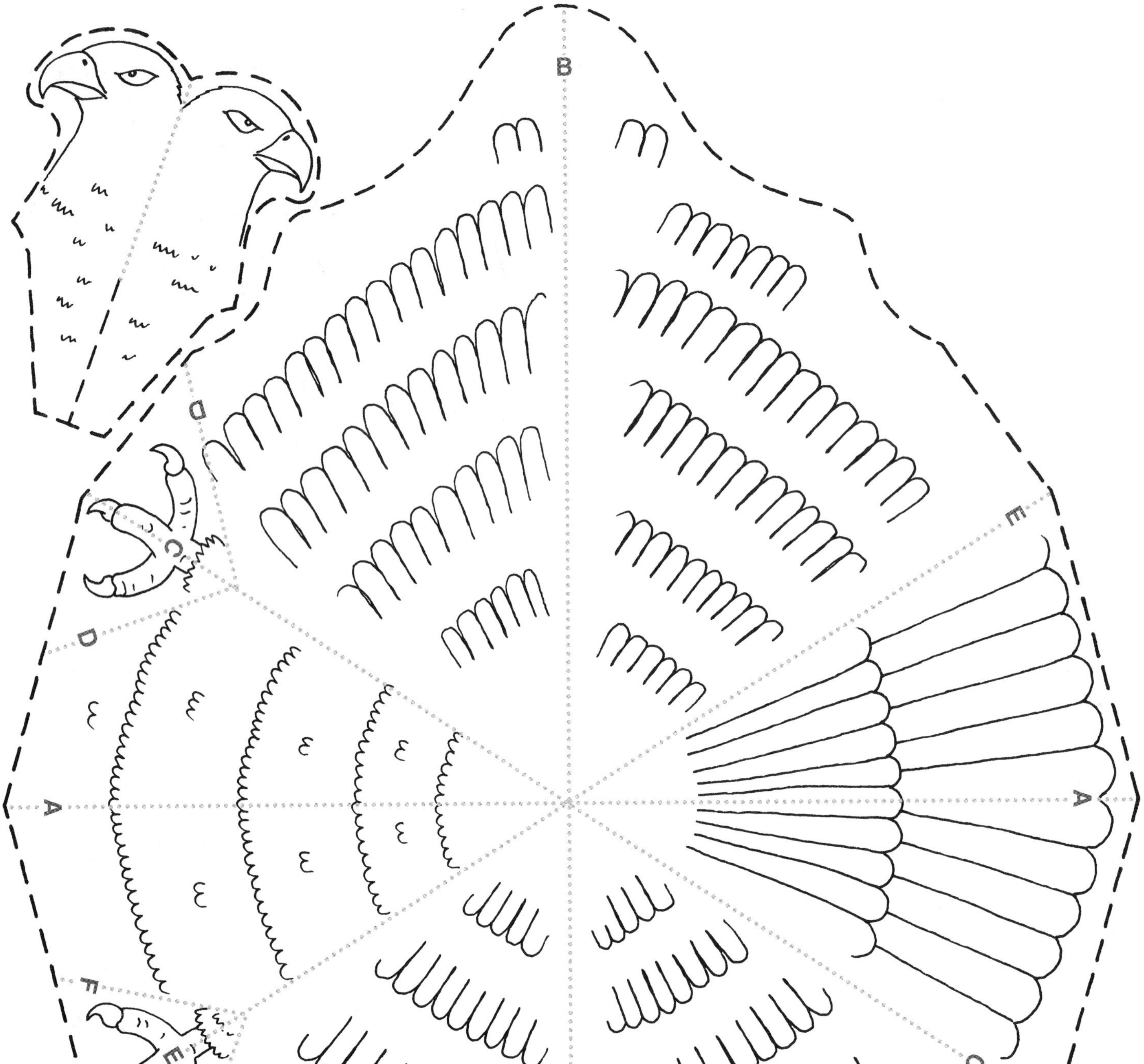
B
D
C
E
D
A
A
F
E
F
C
B

Totem Pole

To the Native Americans, a totem pole was like a lucky charm. They carved pictures on it to help protect themselves from evil. Make this totem pole and decorate it with your own favourite colours and lucky charms.

You will need: the Totem Pole template • scissors • pencil • pencil crayons for decorating

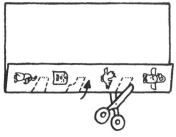

1. Fold the paper backwards along the A dots. Cut along all the dashes.

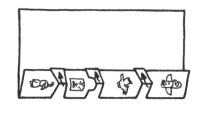

2. Fold the shapes forwards along the dots. Then fold them backwards. Open out the paper.

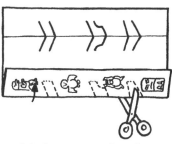

3. Fold the paper backwards along the B dots. Cut along all the dashes. Then repeat step 2.

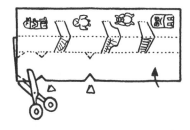

4. Fold backwards along the C dots. Cut along the dashes. Unfold.

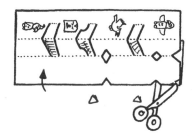

5. Fold backwards along the D dots. Cut along the dashes. Unfold.

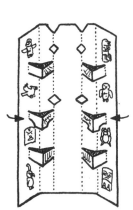

6. Fold forwards along the A and B dots. Pull the pop-up shapes forwards.

7. Fold backwards along the C and D dots. Then stand your model up.

Press your model flat. Do you have a lucky toy or piece of clothing? Draw pictures of your lucky charms. Then tell a friend about the things you have drawn.

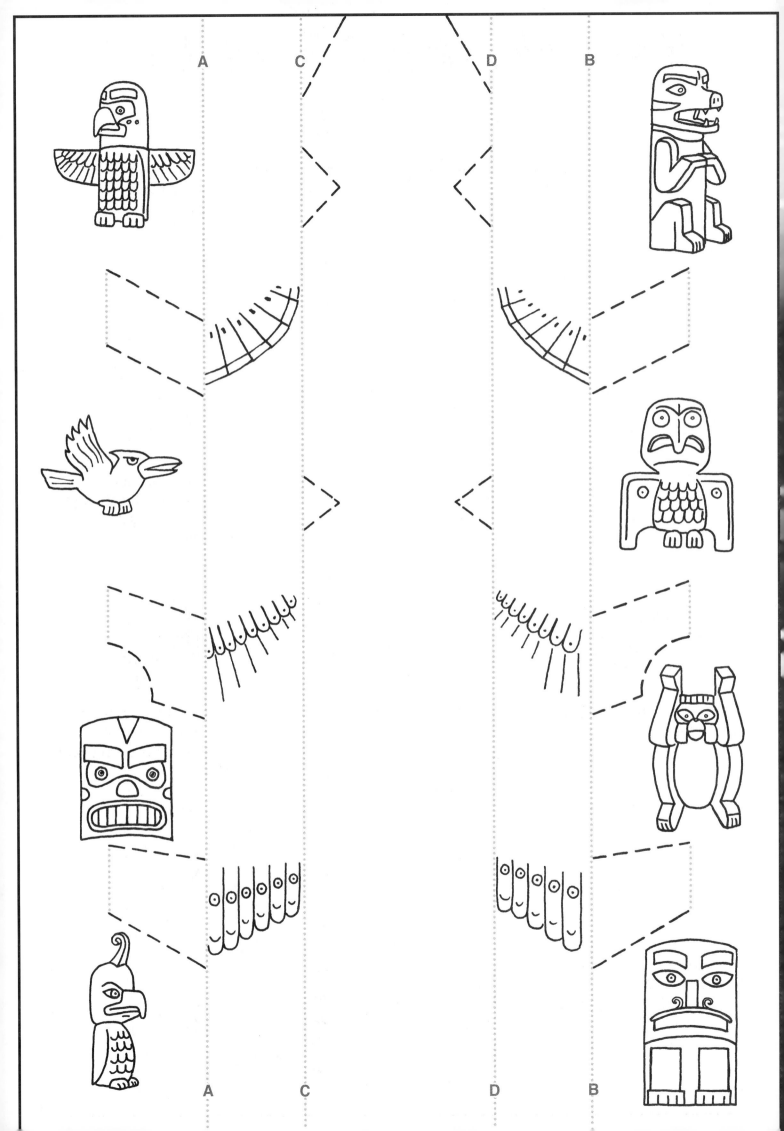

How the Kiwi Bird Lost its Wings

A kiwi is a bird from New Zealand. This story is about why the brave kiwi gave up its wings and went to guard the trees on the forest floor. You can tell the story yourself on this kiwi bird model.

You will need: the How the Kiwi Bird Lost its Wings template
- the story of How the Kiwi Bird Lost its Wings (page 59)
- scissors • pencil • pencil crayons for decorating

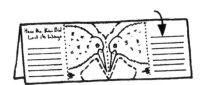

1. Fold the paper in half lengthways, like this.

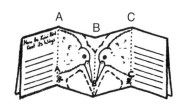

2. Fold the paper in a zig-zag along the dots (A, B, C). Start by folding forwards along the A dots.

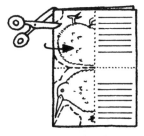

3. Open out the paper fully. Then fold in half widthways, like this. Cut along all the dashes.

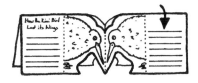

4. Open out the paper. Fold in half lengthways again.

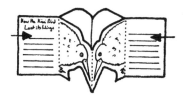

5. Push the left and right edges towards each other, so that you make a box shape in the middle. Keep pushing until the sides touch.

6. Fold backwards along the A and C dots. Then fold forwards. Unfold. Stand your model up.

Read the story. Then press your model flat and write the story in your own words. You could imagine you are the kiwi bird telling the story to your friends. Decorate the picture using pencil crayons.

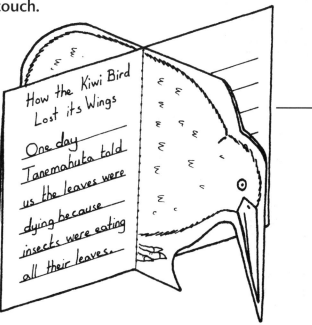

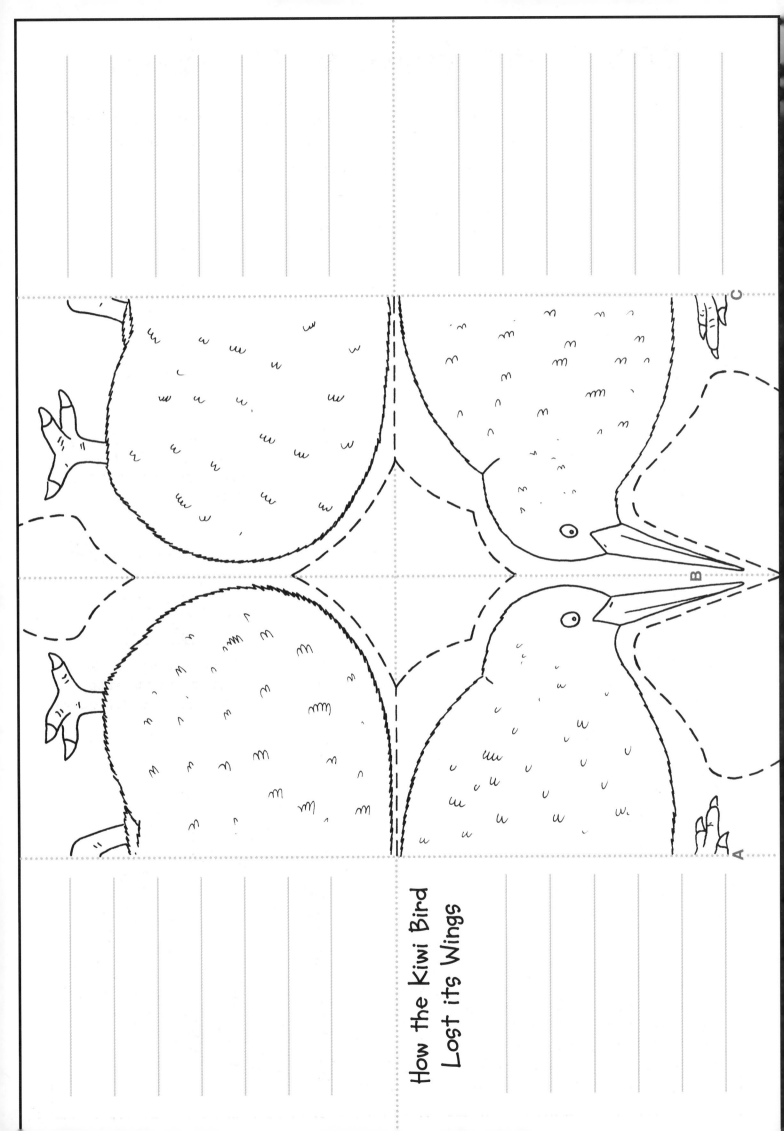

How the Kiwi Bird
Lost its Wings

How the Sun was Made

In this story from Australia, the sun is made from a huge fire. Every day, a good spirit puts more wood on the fire. Make this pop-up card and write your own story of how the sun got into the sky.

You will need: the How the Sun was Made template • scissors • glue • pencil • yellow or orange pencil crayons for decorating

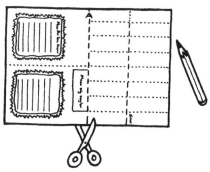

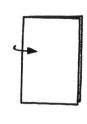

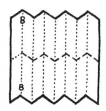

1. Cut along the A dashes. Colour both sides of the piece marked 'SUN' yellow or orange.

2. Fold the other piece of paper in half, like this. Unfold.

3. Fold the sun in a zig-zag along the dots. Start by folding forwards along the B dots.

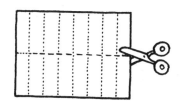

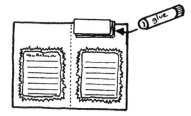

4. Unfold. Cut along the dashes. (Don't cut all the way across!)

5. Fold backwards along the C dots. Glue the end of the zig-zag together, like this.

6. Fold up the zig-zag. Spread glue on the bottom strip. Place the zig-zag on the card.

7. Spread glue on top of the zig-zag. Then fold the card closed and leave it to dry.

When the glue is dry, open your card. Make up a story about how the sun was made. Perhaps the sun is a giant candle or a never-ending firework display? Write your story on the card.

B

SUN

C

B

A ─────────────────────────────────────── A

PLACE ZIG-ZAG HERE

How the Sun was Made

The Poor Fisherman

Long ago, a fisherman and his wife lived in a tiny shack by the sea. One day, the fisherman caught an amazing talking fish.

"Please spare me," begged the fish. "If you let me go, I'll give you three wishes."

The fisherman put the fish back in the water and went home to tell his wife.

The next day, the fisherman went out in his boat and spoke to the fish.

"Oh fish," he said. "My wife wants to live in a little cottage. Please grant her wish."

The fish nodded. When the fisherman went home, he found his wife standing smiling at the door of a little cottage, with a garden filled with flowers and fruit.

But she wasn't happy for long. A few days later, the fisherman went to the sea again.

"Oh fish," he said. "My wife wants to live in a big palace. Please grant her wish."

The fish nodded. And when the fisherman went home, his wife was sitting in a beautiful palace, full of fine furniture.

But she wasn't happy for long. A third time, the fisherman went back to the sea.

"Oh fish," he said. "My wife wants to be queen. Please grant her wish."

The fish nodded. And when the fisherman went home, he found his wife sitting on a golden throne, wearing a golden crown.

But next she wanted to be the richest person in all the world. The fisherman went back to the sea and asked for one more wish.

"Your wife is very greedy," said the fish, angrily. "And your wishes are used up. Go back and live in your shack."

So the fisherman and his wife went back to their shack and were just as poor as ever before. But now they had learned to be happy.

The North Wind and the Sun

The North Wind and the Sun were always quarrelling.

"I'm stronger than you," boasted the North Wind.

"That's not true," said the Sun. "Everyone knows that I'm stronger than you."

"Rubbish," sneered the North Wind. "Let's see if you can prove it."

"Very well," the Sun replied. "Look down there." He pointed to the ground.

Far below, a man was walking along the road. He was wearing a warm, winter coat.

"I can make that man take off his coat," said the Sun. "And I bet you can't."

"Pah! Easy, peasy," sniggered the North Wind.

Then the North Wind blew as hard as he could. He blew the leaves off the trees and the sky filled with dust. But the harder the North Wind blew, the colder the man felt. He wrapped his coat more tightly around him to stop himself from shivering.

Then it was the Sun's turn. He shone gently down on the ground. As it grew warmer, the flowers burst into bloom and birds began to sing. Soon the man felt so hot that he took off his coat and sat down in a shady spot.

"How did you do that?" asked the North Wind, grumpily.

"It was easy," replied the Sun. "While you huffed and puffed, I used gentleness instead."

Androcles and the Lion

There was once a slave called Androcles who was badly treated by his master. Androcles escaped and ran into the forest to hide. There he found a huge lion lying on the ground, groaning. Androcles started to run away, but to his surprise, the lion did not chase after him. Androcles stopped and turned around.

The lion held out its paw, which was swollen and bleeding. There was a large thorn stuck in it. Gently, Androcles pulled out the thorn and bandaged the lion's paw. The lion licked him gratefully and the two became friends.

Not long afterwards, Androcles was caught. As a punishment for running away, he was sentenced to be thrown to a hungry lion. Androcles trembled as the lion was let loose from its den and rushed towards him, roaring. But instead of eating Androcles, the lion began to lick him. For the lion was none other than his friend from the forest.

Seeing what had happened, the emperor took pity on Androcles and set him free. Then Androcles and the friendly lion went off to live in the forest together.

Habeeb and the Flying Carpet

All day long, Habeeb the carpet-maker's son dreamed of going off on an adventure. It made his father very cross.

"You lazy good-for-nothing," his father shouted. "Always day-dreaming when you should be helping me make carpets. Now get back to work!"

But Habeeb wasn't interested in making carpets. One night, he crept out of the house and joined a camel caravan bound for the faraway city of Samarkand. All he took with him was a small carpet he had found in a corner of the shop. It was too old and worn for anyone to miss.

For many days and nights, the camels plodded through baking deserts until they reached Samarkand. That night, Habeeb was too excited to sleep. He sat on his carpet and said,

"I wish this carpet could fly."

No sooner were the words out of his mouth than he was flying through the air on his magic carpet! It carried him off to a beautiful palace. There he met a princess called Golden Flower who asked him to play marbles with her. But when the guards saw Habeeb, they began to chase him away. At once, he jumped onto his carpet and flew back home to his father's house.

Many years later, Habeeb set out to find Princess Golden Flower again. He travelled far and wide, but no one had heard of her.

Then one day, in a far-off land, he heard her name spoken — she was the king's daughter! At last, he'd found her. Soon afterwards, Habeeb and the princess were married. They lived happily ever after.

Ali Baba and the Forty Thieves

Once upon a time, a poor woodcutter called Ali Baba saw forty thieves dashing through the wood. He followed them to a secret cave with a giant stone across the entrance.

"Open sesame," the thieves cried. And the stone rolled away. In the thieves went. Later, when they had left, Ali Baba crept towards the cave.

"Open sesame," he whispered. And the stone rolled away. Inside, Ali Baba couldn't believe his eyes — the cave was piled high with gold! Ali Baba grabbed as much gold as he could carry and ran home.

The next day, Ali Baba went back to get some more gold. But the forty thieves caught sight of him! Realising he had taken their gold, they were filled with rage. They formed a cunning plan. They would sneak into Ali Baba's house and hide in some large storage jars. When Ali Baba came home, they would jump out and attack him.

Luckily, Ali Baba arrived home just in time to see the thieves climbing into the jars. He rolled the jars out of his house and down a steep hill into the river. And the forty thieves were never seen again.

The Clever Jackal

There was once a poor weaver who had a very clever pet jackal. Each night, as the weaver slept, the jackal wove material for his master to turn into fine clothes.

One day, the weaver sighed.

"I am weary," he said to the jackal. "If only we didn't have to work so hard."

The clever jackal had an idea. He took a bundle of the weaver's most beautiful clothes and ran to the royal palace. There he found the princess sitting in the garden.

"Your highness," said the jackal, with a bow. "My master is very rich. He has sent you these fine clothes as a gift."

The princess was delighted. She told her father that she wanted to marry the jackal's rich master.

The jackal ran and told the weaver the good news. Then they worked all day and all night to make the best wedding clothes ever seen. When the weaver tried them on, he looked like a handsome prince.

The jackal asked all the animals in the forest to come to the wedding. Afterwards, it was time to return to the weaver's house. The princess was shocked at how tiny it was. She realised she had married a poor weaver, but she didn't mind. She loved him very much.

The princess and the weaver were happy making clothes together. Now the weaver didn't have to work so hard any more. And so the clever jackal had made the poor weaver's dream come true.

The Honey Bird

In the days when all the animals were friends, there lived a little honey bird. The animals loved honey. And the honey bird knew the best places to find it.

"Cheka, cheka!" it sang. "Follow me, if you want some honey."

One day, a girl out walking heard the honey bird's song.

"I'll follow you," she said to the honey bird. "I'd like some honey."

So the girl and the honey bird set off through the forest. On the way, they met an antelope, a leopard, a zebra and a lion.

"Cheka, cheka!" sang the honey bird. "If you want some honey, follow me."

Before long, the honey bird flew up into a tall tree.

"Cheka, cheka!" it sang. "Here is the sweetest, tastiest honey."

Quick as a flash, the girl climbed the tree and pulled down a big honeycomb. She broke it into pieces and shared it out among the animals. But the animals started to squabble and fight over who had the biggest bit.

The girl was very angry.

"Stop it! Stop it!" she shouted. "Now that you have quarrelled, you will never be friends again."

Then the leopard jumped up and chased away the antelope. The lion gave a roar and chased away the zebra. Only the girl and the honey bird were left.

"Cheka, cheka!" sang the honey bird. "Now we can share our honey in peace."

The Tortoise and the Leopard

A very lazy tortoise loved to eat juicy vegetables. But he was too busy sleeping to grow his own food. And now he was hungry. So he made himself a leopard disguise and set off for the market.

At the market, the frightened shopkeepers thought he was a real leopard. They ran away as fast as they could. Then the tortoise stole their vegetables and munched them greedily.

When the shopkeepers found out that they'd been tricked, they were furious. They decided to teach the tortoise a lesson. So they made a model of a man and stood it in the market place. Then they waited for the tortoise to return.

The next day, the tortoise put on his leopard disguise again and went back to the market. Thinking the model was a real man, he went right up to it and pushed it.

"Why aren't you scared of the leopard?" he demanded. "Why haven't you run away?"

But the shopkeepers had covered the model man with lots of sticky glue. The tortoise was stuck fast to it. He was trapped! The shopkeepers set him free, on one condition — that he never stole from them again.

How the Kiwi Bird Lost its Wings

One day, the god Tanemahuta was walking through the forest. He noticed that the trees were dying because insects were eating their leaves. Whatever could he do to save the trees? He called all the forest birds together and spoke to them.

"Something is eating the trees," he said. "One of you must come and live on the forest floor to guard them. Who will come?"

None of the birds spoke.

Tanemahuta turned to the Tui bird.

"Tui, will you come down from the tree tops?"

The Tui bird looked up at the tree tops and saw the sun shining through the leaves. Then he looked down at the forest floor and saw that it was gloomy and dark.

"I can't," he said, trembling. "I'm scared of the dark."

Then Tanemahuta turned to the Pukeko bird.

"Pukeko, will you come down from the tree tops?"

The Pukeko bird looked up at the tree tops and saw the sun shining through the leaves. Then she looked down at the forest floor and saw that it was mouldy and damp.

"I can't," she said, shuddering. "I don't want to get my feet wet."

Then Tanemahuta turned to the Pipiwharaurao bird.

"Pipiwharaurao, will you come down from the tree tops?"

The Pipiwharaurao bird looked up at the tree tops and saw the sun shining through the leaves. Then he looked down at the forest floor and saw that it was cold and draughty.

"I can't," he said, shivering. "I want to stay in my warm nest."

Tanemahuta felt sad. He knew that if he could not save the trees, all the birds would lose their homes. He turned to the Kiwi bird.

"Kiwi, will you come down from the tree tops?"

The Kiwi bird looked up at the tree tops and saw the sun shining through the leaves. Then she looked down at the forest floor.

"Yes," she said, "I will."

Tanemahuta was overjoyed, but he gave the Kiwi bird a warning.

"If you do this," he said, "you will have to grow thick, strong legs to walk on the ground. You will lose your wings and never return to the tree tops. Will you still come?"

The Kiwi bird took one last look up at the sunshine in the tree tops. She took one last look at the other birds and said a silent goodbye. Then she turned to Tanemahuta.

"Yes, I will," she said, quietly.

And from that day on, the Kiwi bird has never been able to fly. But because of her great bravery, she became the best loved bird of them all.

Helpful hints

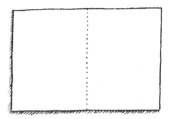 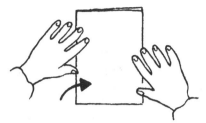

Fold along the **dots**

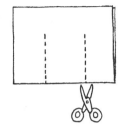

Cut along the **dashes**

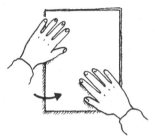 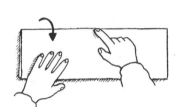

fold **widthways**   fold **lengthways**

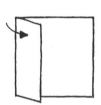 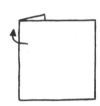

fold **forwards**   fold **backwards**

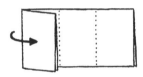 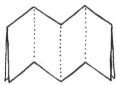

Zig-zag
Fold forwards along the first dotted line.
Fold backwards along the second dotted line.
Fold forwards along the third dotted line.
Continue until you reach the end.

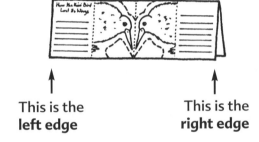

This is the
left edge

This is the
right edge

Using glue

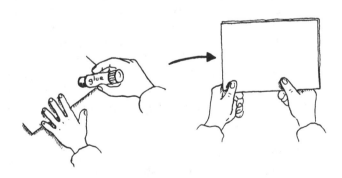

Use very small amounts of glue. Press together
the pieces you have glued to help them stick.

Using scissors

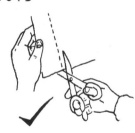

Do not put your hand holding the paper in front of
the scissors.

Close the scissors when you are not using them.

Make sure the scissors don't get hidden under
pieces of paper.

Teachers' notes

by Anita Ganeri

The Sword in the Stone (pages 5–6)

Discuss the story of how King Arthur came by his sword, Excalibur (you could read the story to them — there are many abridged versions available). The semi-historical character of Arthur is said to have led the Britons into battle against the Saxons. The stories about King Arthur were written and developed from the 12th century onwards. In this legend, the king of England died leaving no heir. The sword Excalibur was fixed in a great stone; whoever pulled it out would be king. A young man called Arthur came across the sword while out walking and, without realising its significance, succeeded in pulling it from the stone. He was then made king of England. You could read and act out other stories about King Arthur and the Knights of the Round Table.

Beowulf (pages 7–8)

This Old English poem tells of the hero Beowulf, who in his youth killed a half-human monster called Grendel which was attacking the hall of the Danish king. Beowulf went on to rule over his own kingdom for many years. In his old age he fought the dragon featured in this activity. For centuries the dragon had guarded a great hoard of treasure. One day a thief stole a golden cup from the treasure hoard, rousing the dragon's anger. It flew out of its den and attacked Beowulf's people, threatening to devastate the kingdom. Beowulf and his companion Wiglaf killed the dragon but Beowulf was badly wounded and died of his injuries. After telling the story to the children, encourage them to suggest what they think the dragon looked like. Then ask them to describe what might have happened when Beowulf met the dragon. They could also draw pictures of the monster Grendel. Ask them if they can think of other stories in which dragons appear (such as the legend of Saint George and the dragon). Talk about how dragons are used in stories — often to symbolise evil versus good. To finish off their models, the children could glue scrunched-up red tissue paper in the dragon's mouth for flames.

The Poor Fisherman (pages 9–10)

Give the children copies of the story of The Poor Fisherman (page 55) for them to read and plan their stories. This is a traditional tale from Germany, originally written by the Brothers Grimm (many of the Grimm stories are available in Penguin Classics or on the Internet — see the website contacts). The activity could be linked with text-level work on stories by significant children's authors. After reading the story together, talk to the children about making wishes. Ask them if they have ever made any special wishes in the past and what they would wish for if they were in the poor fisherman's place. Discuss the sort of language that is used to make a wish (for example, *I wish that I had...*, *I would like to...*, *If I had three wishes I would ask for...*). You could encourage the children to write their own version of the story by changing the things the wife wishes for. They could write captions for their pictures. Discuss the moral of the story — that riches do not necessarily bring happiness. Point out that at the end of the story the fisherman's wife has learned to be content with what she has.

Yggdrasil (pages 11–12)

This and the following activity could be linked to history work on the Vikings. Use this project as a focus for talking to the class about myths and legends. It also links to text-level work on oral and performance poetry from different cultures. Explain that myths are stories which are not based in historical fact but use supernatural characters to explain natural events (such as thunder storms, the passage of night and day, and so on). The Viking myths were not written down but passed on by word of mouth. They were retold by skilled storytellers called bards. According to the Yggdrasil myth, the tree held up the earth and its roots reached the world of the gods and other worlds. Ratatösk the squirrel carried insults between the eagle and Nidhogg, the dragon. To extend the storytelling idea, the children could take it in turns to retell the myth of Yggdrasil. Help the children to make up insults for their models by making word banks of adjectives, for example:

Dragon	Eagle
scaly	feathered
spiky	flapping
roaring	screeching

The Rainbow (pages 13–14)

Introduce this activity by talking about the Viking gods and goddesses. The most important god was Odin, who built the great palace of Valhalla in Asgard, the world of the gods. Here the bravest of the Viking warriors killed in battle were chosen to join Odin. A rainbow bridge joined Asgard with the earth, where humans lived. Odin rode an eight-legged horse and had two pet ravens which carried messages for him. Other important gods included Thor, the thunder god, and Njord, god of the sea. Ask the children to look at the picture of Valhalla and to imagine what it looked like inside. For further work on Viking gods and goddesses, ask the children to list words that could be used to describe the different gods (for example, Thor was strong, red-haired and hot-tempered). They could draw a picture of what they imagine one of the gods to look like and add a name label.

The North Wind and the Sun (pages 15–16)

Give the children copies of the story of The North Wind and the Sun (page 55) for them to read and plan what to write in their books. This story is one of Aesop's Fables, which originally come from Greece. Read it with the class and discuss the moral — that gentle persuasion is better than force. Ask the children if they know of any other stories that have a message or teach a lesson. You could read some of the other fables together (in *Aesop's Fables*, Penguin Classics, or see the website contacts) or ask the children to find out about them. You could also discuss real-life situations in which it is better to persuade someone gently than to try to force them to do something.

Androcles and the Lion (pages 17–18)

Give the children copies of the story of Androcles and the Lion (page 56) for them to read and plan what they want to write. Point out that there is not much writing space on the lion model, so they will need to edit the story down to a few sentences. This story is one of Aesop's Fables. After reading it together, discuss the moral of the story — that one good turn deserves another — and talk about the qualities of loyalty and friendship which are brought out in the story. Ask what other qualities the children think are important: for example, generosity, kindness, gentleness and a willingness to share. You could ask the children to plan and write another story based on one of these qualities.

Pandora's Box (pages 19–20)

This and the following three activities could be linked to history work on the ancient Greeks. Before beginning this activity, tell the children the story of Pandora's Box. The story begins with two brothers, Prometheus and Epimetheus, who upset the gods by stealing fire to give to humans (previously humans had been unable to make fires). As a punishment, the gods created a beautiful woman called Pandora and gave her a box which they strictly forbade her to open. Epimetheus married Pandora. But she grew more and more curious about what was inside the box, until one day she opened the lid. Out flew evils such as sickness, misery and death, which have been in the world ever since. But the very last thing to come out of the box was hope, which meant that people should not despair. Hope is represented by a fairy in this project. Ensure that the children write on the paper before assembling the box.

King Midas (pages 21–22)

Tell the children the ancient Greek legend of King Midas. Midas asked the gods to let everything he touched turn to gold. His wish was granted, and at first Midas was delighted. But when he sat down to eat, his food turned to gold as it touched his lips. He had no choice but to ask the gods to release him from his wish. The gods told him to bathe in the river Pactolus and the wish would be undone. Encourage the children to write the story in their books in their own words. Ensure that they write the whole story before they attach the pop-up hand.

Atlantis – the Magical Island (pages 23–24)

Explain to the children that they are going to make a model of Atlantis, a legendary island which, according to the ancient Greeks, was a powerful kingdom thousands of years ago. It had a strong army and its people lived in luxurious palaces and owned fine things. Then, in the space of a day and a night, Atlantis sank beneath the waves. No trace of the island has ever been found and most people doubt if it ever really existed. Ask the children to imagine and describe a beautiful island, with features such as palaces, bridges and gardens. The legend can be linked with text-level work on stories about fantasy worlds; ask the children to make up stories about the people and creatures that lived on the island. The finished island models could be displayed on blue paper to represent the sea.

Medusa (pages 25–26)

First discuss the ancient Greek myth of Medusa. In this story Medusa, the daughter of a sea god, offended Athene, goddess of wisdom. As punishment, she and her two sisters were turned into hideous monsters, with wings, sharp claws, and snakes instead of hair. Anyone who looked into Medusa's eyes was turned to stone. When the children have made the masks, you could organise the class into groups and ask them to act out the story, making up extra details. They will need to allocate the parts of Medusa, her two sisters, Athene and people who are turned to stone. Help them to decide if they need a narrator to tell the story. They could also make masks for the other characters. If they write a playscript for the story, they could first record their ideas for the characters and setting on a chart, for example:

Characters	Setting
Medusa daughter of a sea god Athene goddess of wisdom	ancient Greece a cave by the sea

Habeeb and the Flying Carpet (pages 27–28)

Give the children copies of the story of Habeeb and the Flying Carpet (page 56) and read it with the class. Explain that the story comes from Central Asia and show the children the location of Samarkand (now in Uzbekistan) on a map. Discuss the things Habeeb might have seen on his journey through the desert. Encourage the children to think about where they would like to go if they had a magic carpet. These may be real destinations which you can help the class to plot on a map, or they may be imaginary places. The activity could be linked with non-fiction work on recounts of observations, visits and events. Discuss the type of language and verbs the children will use in their writing: for example, *If I had a flying carpet I would go to...* They may find it helpful to press the boxes flat when gluing on the carpet. The class could make a list of their top five favourite places, with a small description of what each place is like. They could then choose one of these places and write a postcard to send home, describing their visit.

Ali Baba and the Forty Thieves (pages 29–30)

Give the children copies of the story of Ali Baba and the Forty Thieves (page 57) for them to read and plan what they want to write on the jar. After reading the story together, explain that there is only a small amount of space for writing so they will need to pick out the most important parts of the story. This is one of the traditional Oriental tales found in the *Arabian Nights Entertainments* or *The Thousand and One Nights*. It is said that these tales were told nightly by the sultan's new bride, to stave off her execution at daybreak. After a thousand and one nights the sultan relented and agreed not to execute her. You could read some of the other stories to the class (see Penguin Classics or other abridged versions for children).

The Clever Jackal (pages 31–32)

Give the children copies of the story of The Clever Jackal (page 57). Explain that this is a traditional tale from Bengal in north-east India, and show them the location on a map. After reading the story together, ask the children what sort of animal a jackal is and explain that jackals are not found in Britain but are quite common in India. Then talk to the class about what a weaver does and about how cloth and clothes are made. Encourage the children to think about the characters in the story and to make word banks of useful adjectives, for example:

Weaver	Jackal	Princess
hard-working kind	loyal intelligent	beautiful generous

Discuss possible situations and new characters for the children to use in their own stories about the clever jackal.

The Magic Tea Bush (pages 33–34)

Begin the lesson by telling the children the story of The Magic Tea Bush. In this story from China, an old Buddhist monk became so tired that he could not stay awake, even during the day. He missed saying his prayers and felt very ashamed of himself. But the Buddha forgave him and tried to help him. He made a bush spring up from the soil, which was different from any other plant the monk had seen. Whenever the monk was tired, the Buddha said, he should put some of the leaves in hot water to make a refreshing drink. The monk did just this, and immediately was no longer sleepy. He took seeds from the tea bush and spent the rest of his life growing new tea bushes all over China. According to Buddhist legend, this is how people first grew and drank tea. Show the children pictures of China and help them to locate it on a map. You could also explain that the Buddha was a teacher who helped people in suffering and spread the message that people should be content with their lot. He was the founder of the religion Buddhism; however, it is important to make the point that he is not worshipped as a god.

The Herb Fairy (pages 35–36)

Before the children make their books, tell them the story of The Herb Fairy, a traditional tale from south-west China. Legend says that the fairy was once a beautiful young girl who used healing herbs to cure sick people and animals. Then she went to live in the mountains, where to this day she looks after all the herbs that grow there. It is said that if a good, honest person climbs the mountain, the herb fairy will show him or her where to find a precious herb on the mountainside. Talk to the children about how they will decide what to write next to each picture in their book, for example:

Pages 1–2	a description of the herb fairy
Pages 3–4	an honest girl climbs the mountain to look for some healing herbs
Pages 5–7	the herb fairy helps the girl to find some herbs

The Sky God (page 37–38)

Introduce this activity by telling the class this African creation story. Before the beginning of the world, Nyame, the sky god, lived alone in the sky. One day he created the earth; then he took a basket, filled it with plants and animals and lowered it down to earth on a rope. Nyame made a trapdoor in the sky so that he could look down at the earth. One day Nyame was looking through the trapdoor when he suddenly sneezed. Two spirits fell out of his mouth and tumbled down to earth. This was how the first people came to be. During the last stage of making the model, some children may need help with tying the thread. You could give the children creation stories from other cultures for them to read and compare. Encourage them to talk about similarities and differences between the stories.

The Honey Bird (pages 39–40)

Give the children copies of the story of The Honey Bird (page 58). First explain that this is a traditional story from Africa. Help the children to locate Africa on a map of the world, and show them pictures of animals found there which do not live in Britain. Read the story with the children before they make the model. To extend the activity, the children could draw pictures of the girl and the animals in the story. These could be glued onto a background showing an African forest to make a story frieze. The children could then take it in turns to retell different parts of the story to the class.

The Tortoise and the Leopard (pages 41–42)

Give the children copies of the story of The Tortoise and the Leopard (page 58) and read it together before they make the model. Discuss ideas for parts of the story the children could choose to illustrate, and possible captions. To develop the activity, the children could create a cartoon strip to retell the whole story. Discuss how they could divide the story into frames and what text and pictures would go in each frame. Encourage the children to imagine what the characters might be saying or thinking in each frame, and to put these words in speech or thought bubbles.

Ra, the Sun God (pages 43–44)

To introduce this activity, tell the children the ancient Egyptian legend of Ra, the Sun God. Every day Ra sailed across the sky in his boat, pursued by a huge crocodile. At the end of the day, the crocodile seemed to eat up Ra (the sun). However, in the morning the sun reappeared — a sign that Ra had overcome the crocodile. Talk to the children about how the ancient Egyptians used stories like this to explain natural phenomena which they did not understand scientifically, such as how the sun rose and set. This project could be linked to history work on the ancient Egyptians.

The Heavenly Llama (pages 45–46)

Before beginning this activity, show the children pictures of llamas and explain their importance in parts of South America for transport, wool, milk and meat. Encourage the children to think of other animals that are used in similar ways, such as camels, goats and horses. Tell the children the Inca myth of The Heavenly Llama: each night a llama, Yacana, came down from the heavens and drank lots of water from the rivers. If the llama did not do this, the rivers would overflow and the valleys and villages would be flooded.

The Thunderbird (pages 47—48) and
Totem Pole (pages 49—50)

These two stories are based on the myths of the Native Americans. First briefly explain to the class the history of the Native Americans and talk about how important animals were in their culture. Every clan had its own animal founder which was often carved on the clan's totem poles. These animals included ravens, mink, eagles and bears, and were worshipped as guardian spirits. Birds were thought to be powerful spirits; the Thunderbird was a winged god which caused thunder and lightning as it whirled in the sky. Show the children photographs of totem poles and discuss the pictures that were carved on them to ward off bad luck. Then ask the children to talk about their own 'lucky' possessions or mascots. You could ask them to bring an object to school to talk about in front of the class. Invite them to explain the story of the object and why it is important to them.

How the Kiwi Bird Lost its Wings
(pages 51—52)

Give the children copies of the story of How the Kiwi Bird Lost its Wings (page 59) for them to read and plan what they want to write on their models. Before reading the story together, show the children pictures of kiwi birds and explain that they live in New Zealand, where this story comes from. Locate New Zealand on a map of the world. Encourage them to think about different ways of telling the story: for example, in the first person. They might want to tell it from the kiwi bird's point of view or from the point of view of the god Tanemahuta. Ask the children if they can think of any other birds that cannot fly, such as penguins, ostriches and emus; as a further activity, they could choose one of these birds and make up a story about how it lost its wings.

How the Sun was Made (pages 53—54)

First tell the children the Aboriginal myth of How the Sun was Made. The story goes that long ago, before people came to live on earth, there was no sun and the world was dark and cold. Dineewan the emu and Brolga the crane had a fight, during which Brolga snatched one of Dineewan's eggs and flung it high into the sky. The egg smashed open and the bright yellow yolk spilled out. The yolk landed on some firewood, which burst into flames. When a good spirit saw the fire in the sky, he decided to keep it burning, and each morning stoked it with new firewood so that it would light up the earth. You could ask the children to compare this story with that of Ra, the Sun God, which also explains how the sun rises and sets. Encourage them to think about other ways in which the sun could have been created (for example, as a giant candle or a firework display in the sky). To display the finished project, gently bend the crease in the base the opposite way to make the card stay open. You could photocopy the bottom half of the template onto card and the top half onto paper to strengthen the model.

Useful contacts

You and your class can find extra ideas, story texts and pictures for the projects in this book by visiting the following websites.

Websites

www.storyarts.org
   Resources for teachers, including story-related activities, projects and games.
www.english-zone.com
   Texts of Aesop's Fables and resources for teachers.
http://teacher.scholastic.com
   Resources and activities linked to myths, folk tales and fairy tales; also tips for retelling traditional stories and writing workshops.
www.kingarthursknights.com
   Information about King Arthur — the legend and the history.
www.nationalgeographic.com/grimm
   Retellings of 12 Grimm fairy tales with audio and interactive elements.

www.grimmfairytales.com
   Biographies of and stories by the Brothers Grimm.
www.aesopfables.com
   An online collection of over 600 fables.
www.fables.org.uk
   Retellings of selected Aesop's Fables.
www.artsmia.org/world-myths
   Information about world myths and related art and artefacts to explore.
www.mythweb.com
   All about the heroes, gods and monsters of Greek mythology.
www.pitt.edu/~dash/folktexts.html
   A wide range of folklore and mythology texts.
www.pantheon.org
   An online encyclopedia of mythology, folklore and legend.